THE VIETNAM WAR

Opposing Viewpoints

THE VIETNAM WAR

Opposing Viewpoints

David L. Bender

Greenhaven Press

577 Shoreview Park Road
St. Paul, Minnesota 55112

84-01570

Library of Congress Cataloging in Publication Data
Main entry under title:

The Vietnam war.

(Opposing viewpoints series)
Bibliography: p.
Includes index.
1. Vietnam Conflict, 1961-1975—Addresses, essays, lectures. 2. United States—Foreign policy—1945-
—Addresses, essays, lectures. I. Bender, David L.,
1936-   . II. Series.
DS558.2.V54 1984   959.704'3   84-13628
ISBN O-89908-349-8 (lib. bdg.)
ISBN O-89908-324-2 (pbk.)

"Congress shall make no law... abridging the freedom of speech, or of the press."

first amendment to the U.S. Constitution

The basic foundation of our democracy is the first amendment guarantee of freedom of expression. The *Opposing Viewpoints Series* is dedicated to the concept of this basic freedom and the idea that it is more important to practice it than to enshrine it.

Contents

Why Consider Opposing Viewpoints?

"It is better to debate a question without settling it than to settle a question without debating it."

Joseph Joubert (1754-1824)

The Importance of Examining Opposing Viewpoints

The purpose of the Opposing Viewpoints Series, and this book in particular, is to present balanced, and often difficult to find, opposing points of view on complex and sensitive issues.

Probably the best way to become informed is to analyze the positions of those who are regarded as experts and well studied on issues. It is important to consider every variety of opinion in an attempt to determine the truth. Opinions from the mainstream of society should be examined. But also important are opinions that are considered radical, reactionary, or minority as well as those stigmatized by some other uncomplimentary label. An important lesson of history is the eventual acceptance of many unpopular and even despised opinions. The ideas of Socrates, Jesus, and Galileo are good examples of this.

Readers will approach this book with their own opinions on the issues debated within it. However, to have a good grasp of one's own viewpoint, it is necessary to understand the arguments of those with whom one disagrees. It can be said that those who do not completely understand their adversary's point of view do not fully understand their own.

A persuasive case for considering opposing viewpoints has been presented by John Stuart Mill in his work *On Liberty*. When examining controversial issues it may be helpful to reflect on his suggestion:

> The only way in which a human being can make some approach to knowing the whole of a subject, is by hearing what can be said about it by persons of every variety of opinion, and studying all modes in which it can be looked at by every character of mind. No wise man ever acquired his wisdom in any mode but this.

Analyzing Sources of Information

The Opposing Viewpoints Series includes diverse materials taken from magazines, journals, books, and newspapers, as well as statements and position papers from a wide range of individuals, organizations and governments. This broad spectrum of sources helps to develop patterns of thinking which are open to the consideration of a variety of opinions.

Pitfalls to Avoid

A pitfall to avoid in considering opposing points of view is that of regarding one's own opinion as being common sense and the most rational stance and the point of view of others as being only opinion and naturally wrong. It may be that another's opinion is correct and one's own is in error.

Another pitfall to avoid is that of closing one's mind to the opinions of those with whom one disagrees. The best way to approach a dialogue is to make one's primary purpose that of understanding the mind and arguments of the other person and not that of enlightening him or her with one's own solutions. More can be learned by listening than speaking.

It is my hope that after reading this book the reader will have a deeper understanding of the issues debated and will appreciate the complexity of even seemingly simple issues on which good and honest people disagree. This awareness is particularly important in a democratic society such as ours where people enter into public debate to determine the common good. Those with whom one disagrees should not necessarily be regarded as enemies, but perhaps simply as people who suggest different paths to a common goal.

Developing Basic Reading and Thinking Skills

In this book carefully edited opposing viewpoints are purposely placed back to back to create a running debate; each viewpoint is preceeded by a short quotation that best expresses the author's main argument. This format instantly plunges the reader into the midst of a controversial issue and greatly aids that reader in mastering the basic skill of recognizing an author's point of view.

A number of basic skills for critical thinking are practiced in the activities that appear throughout the books in the series. Some of the skills are:

Evaluating Sources of Information   The ability to choose from among alternative sources the most reliable and accurate source in relation to a given subject.

Separating Fact from Opinion   The ability to make the basic distinction between factual statements (those that can be demonstrated or verified empirically) and statements of opinion (those that are beliefs or attitudes that cannot be proved).

Identifying Stereotypes   The ability to identify oversimplified, exaggerated descriptions (favorable or unfavorable) about people and insulting statements about racial, religious or national groups, based upon misinformation or lack of information.

Recognizing Ethnocentrism   The ability to recognize attitudes or opinions that express the view that one's own race, culture, or group is inherently superior, or those attitudes that judge another culture or group in terms of one's own.

It is important to consider opposing viewpoints and equally important to be able to critically analyze those viewpoints. The activities in this book are designed to help the reader master these thinking skills. Statements are taken from the book's viewpoints and the reader is asked to analyze them. This technique aids the reader in developing skills that not only can be applied to the viewpoints in this book, but also to situations where opinionated spokespersons comment on controversial issues. Although the activities are helpful to the solitary reader, they are most useful when the reader can benefit from the interaction of group discussion.

Using this book and others in the series should help readers develop basic reading and thinking skills. These skills should improve the reader's ability to understand what they read. Readers should be better able to separate fact from opinion, substance from rhetoric and become better consumers of information in our media-centered culture.

This volume of the Opposing Viewpoints Series does not advocate a particular point of view. Quite the contrary! The very nature of the book leaves it to the reader to formulate the opinions he or she find most suitable. My purpose as publisher is to see that this is made possible by offering a wide range of viewpoints which are fairly presented.

David L. Bender
Publisher

11

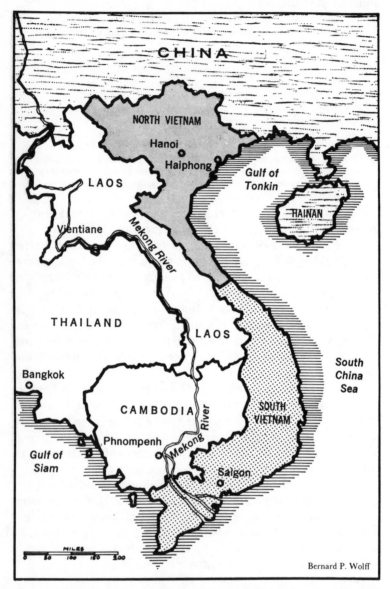

The 1954 Geneva agreements ended 60 years of French occupation and temporarily partitioned Vietnam at the 17th parallel.

Introduction

"Woe to the statesman whose reasons for entering a war do not appear so plausible at its end as at its beginning."

Otto von Bismarck (1815-1898)

In July 1962, Nikita Khrushchev, Premier of the USSR, remarked to the American ambassador Llewellyn Thompson: "In South Vietnam, the United States has stumbled into a bog. It will be mired down there a long time." Khrushchev's words clearly moved beyond prophesy as the United States ultimately found itself involved in an Asian land war which it could neither seem to win nor honorably abandon. What began as a very limited effort to check Communist expansion in South Vietnam, ended over a decade later with more than 200,000 American soldiers killed or wounded. And beyond this calamitous legacy in human lives, what remains is perhaps the most disfigured chapter in American military and diplomatic history.

US involvement in Vietnam began during the administration of Dwight D. Eisenhower (1953-1960). Vietnam, a former French colony, had been partitioned in 1954 into a Communist-dominated regime in the north and an anti-Communist regime in the south. North Vietnam, under the leadership of the skilled guerilla fighter Ho Chi Minh, was lending military support to a group of Communist insurgents in the south who were attempting to overthrow the South Vietnamese government. Under Eisenhower, several hundred military advisors were sent, along with economic aid, to strengthen the forces of anti-Communism. However, as the insurgency began making consequential inroads, Eisenhower's successor, John F. Kennedy (1961-1963), decided to commit American support troops to South Vietnam.

A Half Million Troops

In 1962, 4,000 troops were sent. Moreover, the United States began involving itself directly in the political affairs of South Vietnam, at first supporting and then contributing to the overthrow of the repressive regime of President Ngo Dinh Diem in 1963. From that point on, events moved swiftly as US intervention mushroomed both politically and militarily. In 1964, President Lyndon B. Johnson (1963-1968) ordered US air strikes against North Vietnam. By 1965, these air strikes had become an almost daily part of the war. The number of American ground troops also increased significantly. In 1966, 200,000 US soldiers were fighting in Vietnam. That number grew annually until by 1969, over a half million troops were committed to the Vietnam enterprise.

Initially, most Americans backed Washington's Vietnam policy. Government reports depicted the Viet Cong (the name given the Communist insurgents) as a Communist guerilla movement which employed terror and coercion to force the hapless peasantry of South Vietnam into submission. Moreover, the North Vietnamese, who were underwriting the efforts of the Viet Cong with troops and armaments, were receiving a steady supply of war materials and monies from Communist bloc nations, especially the People's Republic of China. A dangerous situation seemed to be developing, one which the US government referred to as the "Domino Theory": If South Vietnam were allowed to fall to Communism, so eventually would the rest of southeast Asia. Given these circumstances, aiding the government of South Vietnam appeared both honorable and consistent with America's best interests. But as the war dragged on and a military victory appeared more and more elusive, these arguments rapidly were becoming moot. Much weightier arguments were evolving, namely the cost in American/Vietnamese lives and American dollars. And of greater consequence, Americans began questioning the credibility of those factors allegedly motivating their government's involvement.

A National Debate

The final outcome was a national debate which was substantively unlike any ever witnessed in America. The war prompted many to examine the ultimate sources and grounds of American democracy. For the first time, the morality and designs of an American military involvement were seriously questioned on a large and telling scale. Throughout the nation, from all quarters, the same questions were being asked with growing regularity. Was the cause of freedom at home and in the world really being served in Vietnam or had the government created a self-serving illusion? Did America possess the economic and military resources to oversee world freedom; and, more basically, did it hold the moral right? As a final scathing indictment, was American interventionism abroad anything but hypocritical so long as the nation continued to ally with and even actively support dictatorial regimes whose dubious saving grace was their opposition to communism? In less than a decade, Vietnam, a nation which in 1960 was practically unknown to most Americans, succeeded in generating the greatest amount of domestic unrest experienced in the United States since the Civil War.

Predictably, Vietnam became the primary focus of attention during the presidential election of 1968. In an apparent effort to induce the North Vietnamese to join the US in negotiating a settlement to the war, President Johnson announced that he would not seek re-election. His vice-president, Hubert H. Humphrey, became the Democratic nominee and was defeated by Richard M. Nixon (1969-1974) who claimed to have a "secret plan" for honorably disengaging American troops. However, Nixon's "secret plan," which amounted to a greater South Vietnamese troop involvement in concert with a gradual American pullout, in many respects succeeded only in intensifying the conflict.

US participation in the war ultimately ended in March 1973 following several years of peace negotiations. However, America's reaction to the new-found peace was more of pain than relief as North Vietnam quickly and decisively exploited the void left by the United States. The Communists persisted with a new tenacity as hamlet after hamlet, city after city, methodically fell to their forces. Gerald Ford (1974-1976), who succeeded Richard Nixon when the latter resigned in the wake of the Watergate scandal, attempted unsuccessfully to secure additional military aid from Congress for South Vietnam. Congress and the nation were little disposed toward repeating what were perceived as past errors. Finally, in April 1975 Communist forces captured Saigon, the capital of South Vietnam and renamed it Ho Chi Minh City after North Vietnam's late and revered leader. What remained was the stinging realization that a dozen years of American financial and military might had accomplished little more than prolong the inevitable.

The Aftermath

It is difficult to exaggerate the consequences of Vietnam. The conflict has become a festering wound upon the American body politic and it refuses to heal. Since 1973, hardly a year has passed when Americans are not reminded of that war which they neither lost nor won. Indeed, Vietnam has become a virtual metaphor for any questionable or unwinnable military adventure. The 1979 Soviet invasion of Afghanistan, while sparking indignant outcries throughout much of the world, also illuminated smug and knowing smiles as most felt certain that Afghanistan would soon become Moscow's Vietnam. In Washington, the "metaphor" seems to have contributed to the somewhat cautionary reaction to the current Central American situation. The prospect of another Vietnam—no-matter how weak the comparison—has become the nightmare of Americans. In fact, some might argue that therein lies Vietnam's greatest, and perhaps only, positive consequence.

This anthology of opposing viewpoints traces Vietnam from the earliest days of US involvement through the comparisons with Central America today. The topics debated include: Why Did the US Become Involved in Vietnam? Why Did US Policy Fail in Vietnam? What Are the Consequences of Vietnam? What Are the Lessons of Vietnam? and Is Central America Another Vietnam? A chapter by chapter periodical bibliography, an annotated book bibliography, and a chronology of events are included to assist those readers interested in further research. Finally, a series of discussion activities are offered which the editor believes will help actively involve the reader in many of the decision-making processes which contributed to the Vietnam experience. As with all volumes in the Opposing Viewpoints Series, *The Vietnam War* endeavors to achieve editorial objectivity. The editor's role is merely to present a wide spectrum of opinions regarding US involvement in Vietnam. Conclusions to be reached from reading and evaluating these diverse opinions are the responsibility of the reader.

Why Did the US Become Involved in Vietnam?

"If the Communist forces won uncontested control over Indochina or any substantial part thereof, they would surely resume the same pattern of aggression against other free peoples in the area."

The US Must Stop Communist Expansion (1954)

John Foster Dulles

John Foster Dulles served as Secretary of State from 1953 to 1959 under President Eisenhower. One of the primary architects of America's post-World War Two anticommunist policy, he regarded communism as a moral evil to be forcefully opposed. He supported the Nationalist Chinese against Communist China and was a strong backer of the South Vietnamese government of Ngo Dinh Diem. In the following viewpoint Secretary Dulles presents an early argument for US involvement in Vietnam that other proponents for US involvement would later build on.

As you read, consider the following questions:

1. Secretary Dulles claims the communists have a plan, under the leadership of Ho Chi Minh, for amalgamating Indochina into the Soviet orbit. What is the plan he identifies?
2. How does Secretary Dulles suggest communist control of Indochina would affect the interests of the US and its allies?

John Foster Dulles, from a speech delivered to the Overseas Press Club of America, New York, March 29, 1954.

Indochina is important for many reasons. First—and always first—are the human values. About 30 million people are seeking for themselves the dignity of self-government. Until a few years ago, they formed merely a French dependency. Now, their three political units—Vietnam, Laos and Cambodia—are exercising a considerable measure of independent political authority within the French Union. Each of the three is now recognized by the United States and by more than 30 other nations. They signed the Japanese Peace Treaty with us. Their independence is not yet complete. But the French Government last July declared its intention to complete that independence, and negotiations to consummate that pledge are actively under way.

The United States is watching this development with close attention and great sympathy. We do not forget that we were a colony that won its freedom. We have sponsored in the Philippines a conspicuously successful development of political independence. We feel a sense of kinship with those everywhere who yearn for freedom.

The Communist Plan

The Communists are attempting to prevent the orderly development of independence and to confuse the issue before the world. The Communists have, in these matters, a regular line which Stalin laid down in 1924.

The scheme is to whip up the spirit of nationalism so that it becomes violent. That is done by professional agitators. Then the violence is enlarged by Communist military and technical leadership and the provision of military supplies. In these ways, international Communism gets a strangle hold on the people and it uses that power to "amalgamate" the peoples into the Soviet orbit. "Amalgamation" is Lenin's and Stalin's word to describe their process.

"Amalgamation" is now being attempted in Indochina under the ostensible leadership of Ho Chi Minh. He was indoctrinated in Moscow. He became an associate of the Russian, Borodin [Mikhail Markovich Grusenberg], when the latter was organizing the Chinese Communist Party which was to bring China into the Soviet orbit. Then Ho transferred his activities to Indochina.

Those fighting under the banner of Ho Chi Minh have largely been trained and equipped in Communist China. They are supplied with artillery and ammunition through the Soviet-Chinese Communist block. Captured materiel shows that much of it was fabricated by the Skoda Munition Works in Czechoslovakia and transported across Russia and Siberia and then sent through China into Vietnam. Military supplies for the Communist armies have been pouring into Vietnam at a steadily increasing rate.

Military and technical guidance is supplied by an estimated 2,000

19

Communist Chinese. They function with the forces of Ho Chi Minh in key positions—in staff sections of the high command, at the division level and in specialized units such as signal, engineer, artillery and transportation.

In the present stage, the Communists in Indochina use nationalistic anti-French slogans to win local support. But if they achieved military or political success, it is certain that they would subject the people to a cruel Communist dictatorship taking its orders from Peiping and Moscow.

The Scope of the Danger

The tragedy would not stop there. If the Communist forces won uncontested control over Indochina or any substantial part thereof, they would surely resume the same pattern of aggression against other free peoples in the area.

The propagandists of Red China and Russia make it apparent that the purpose is to dominate all of Southeast Asia.

Grave View of Communist Aggression

The President, in his April 16, 1953, address, and I myself in an address of Sept. 2, 1953, made clear that the United States would take a grave view of any future overt military Chinese Communist aggression in relation to the Pacific or Southeast Asia area. Such an aggression would threaten island and peninsular positions which secure the United States and its allies.

If such overt military aggression occurred, that would be a deliberate threat to the United States itself. The United States would, of course, invoke the processes of the United Nations and consult with its allies. But we could not escape ultimate responsibility for decisions closely touching our own security and self-defense.

John Foster Dulles, speech, June 11, 1954.

Southeast Asia is the so-called "rice bowl" which helps to feed the densely populated region that extends from India to Japan. It is rich in many raw materials, such as tin, oil, rubber, and iron ore. It offers industrial Japan potentially important markets and sources of raw materials.

The area has great strategic value. Southeast Asia is astride the most direct and best developed sea and air routes between the Pacific and South Asia. It has major naval and air bases. Communist control of Southeast Asia would carry a grave threat to the Philippines, Australia and New Zealand, with whom we have treaties of mutual assistance. The entire Western Pacific area, including the so-called "offshore island chain," would be strategically endangered.

20

President Eisenhower appraised the situation last Wednesday when he said that the area is of "transcendent importance."

The United States Position

The United States has shown in many ways its sympathy for the gallant struggle being waged in Indochina by French forces and those of the Associated States. Congress has enabled us to provide material aid to the established governments and their peoples. Also, our diplomacy has sought to deter Communist China from open aggression in that area.

President Eisenhower, in his address of April 16, 1953, explained that a Korean armistice would be a fraud if it merely released aggressive armies for attack elsewhere. I said last September that if Red China sent its own Army into Indochina, that would result in grave consequences which might not be confined to Indochina.

Recent statements have been designed to impress upon potential aggressors that aggression might lead to action at places and by means of free-world choosing, so that aggression would cost more than it could gain.

The Chinese Communists have, in fact, avoided the direct use of their own Red armies in open aggression against Indochina. They have, however, largely stepped up their support of the aggression in that area. Indeed, they promote that aggression by all means short of open invasion.

Under all the circumstances it seems desirable to clarify further the United States position.

Under the conditions of today, the imposition on Southeast Asia of the political system of Communist Russia and its Chinese Communist ally, by whatever means, would be a grave threat to the whole free community. The United States feels that that possibility should not be passively accepted, but should be met by united action. This might involve serious risks. But these risks are far less than those that will face us a few years from now, if we dare not be resolute today.

The free nations want peace. However, peace is not had merely by wanting it. Peace has to be worked for and planned for. Sometimes it is necessary to take risks to win peace just as it is necessary in war to take risks to win victory. The chances for peace are usually bettered by letting a potential aggressor know in advance where his aggression could lead him.

"To pour money, materiel, and men into the jungles of Indochina without at least a remote prospect of victory would be dangerously futile and self-destructive."

The US Must Be Cautious (1954)

John F. Kennedy

John F. Kennedy was President of the United States from 1961 until his assassination in November 1963. Although Mr. Kennedy was to eventually send several thousand US advisory troops to Vietnam during his presidency, in the following viewpoint he argues for caution and restraint. In his speech, made during the time he was a US Senator, Mr. Kennedy claims that political independence for the Vietnamese people should be the cornerstone of future US policy in Indochina. He warns against the folly of military involvement in the jungles of Indochina.

As you read, consider the following questions:

1. Why does Senator Kennedy argue for a closer examination of the Indochina situation before American involvement?
2. Why is the senator critical of optimistic US statements concerning French military success in Indochina?
3. What is the primary reason the senator gives for claiming that American military assistance would be unproductive?

John F. Kennedy, speech to the US Senate, April 6, 1954.

The time has come for the American people to be told the blunt truth about Indochina.

US Must Examine Situation

I am reluctant to make any statement which may be misinterpreted as unappreciative of the gallant French struggle at Dien Bien Phu and elsewhere; or as partisan criticism of our Secretary of State just prior to his participation in the delicate deliberations in Geneva. Nor, as one who is not a member of those committees of the Congress which have been briefed—if not consulted—on this matter, do I wish to appear impetuous or an alarmist in my evaluation of the situation. But the speeches of President Eisenhower, Secretary Dulles, and others have left too much unsaid, in my opinion—and what has been left unsaid is the heart of the problem that should concern every citizen. For if the American people are, for the fourth time in this century, to travel the long and tortuous road of war—particularly a war which we now realize would threaten the survival of civilization—then I believe we have a right—a right which we should have hitherto exercised—to inquire in detail into the nature of the struggle in which we may become engaged, and the alternative to such struggle. Without such clarification the general support and success of our policy is endangered.

The Geneva Negotiations

Inasmuch as Secretary Dulles has rejected, with finality, any suggestion of bargaining on Indochina in exchange for recognition of Red China, those discussions in Geneva which concern that war may center around two basic alternatives:

The first is a negotiated peace, based either upon partition of the area between the forces of the Viet Minh and the French Union, possibly along the 16th parallel; or based upon a coalition government in which Ho Chi Minh is represented. Despite any wishful thinking to the contrary, it should be apparent that the popularity and prevalence of Ho Chi Minh and his following throughout Indochina would cause either partition or a coalition government to result in eventual domination by the Communists.

The second alternative is for the United States to persuade the French to continue their valiant and costly struggle; an alternative which, considering the current state of opinion in France, will be adopted only if the United States pledges increasing support. Secretary Dulles' statement that the "imposition in southeast Asia of the political system of Communist Russia and its Chinese Communist ally . . . should be met by united action" indicates that it is our policy to give such support; that we will, as observed by the *New York Times* last Wednesday, "fight if necessary to keep southeast Asia out of their hands"; and that we hope to win the support of the free countries of Asia for united action against communism in Indochina, in spite of the fact that such nations have pursued since the war's inception a policy of cold neutrality. . . .

Certainly, I, for one, favor a policy of a "united action" by many nations whenever necessary to achieve a military and political victory for the free world in that area, realizing full well that it may eventually require some commitment of our manpower.

But to pour money, materiel, and men into the jungles of Indochina without at least a remote prospect of victory would be dangerously futile and self-destructive. . . .

Dangers of Intervention

If the present primarily military approach is persisted in, we are likely to be drawn ever more deeply into a Korean-type war, fought under political and military conditions much more unfavorable than those that prevailed in Korea and in the world a decade ago. Such a war cannot be won quickly, if it can be won at all, and may well last, like its Greek and Malayan counterparts, five or ten years, perhaps only to end again in a stalemate, as did the Korean war. . . .

The choices before us are not between intervention and nonintervention, but between an intervention which serves our political interests and thereby limits our military commitments, and an intervention which supports to the bitter end the powers-that-be, even if their policies, by being counterproductive, jeopardize the interests of the United States.

Hans J. Morgenthau, *Commentary*, May 1962.

In February of this year, Defense Secretary Wilson said that a French victory was "both possible and probable" and that the war was going "fully as well as we expected it to at this stage. I see no reason to think Indochina would be another Korea." Also in February of this year, Under Secretary of State Smith stated that:

> The military situation in Indochina is favorable. . . . Contrary to some reports, the recent advances made by the Viet Minh are largely "real estate" operations. . . . Tactically, the French position is solid and the officers in the field seem confident of their ability to deal with the situation.

Less than 2 weeks ago, Admiral Radford, Chairman of the Joint Chiefs of Staff, stated that "the French are going to win." And finally, in a press conference some days prior to his speech to the Overseas Press Club in New York, Secretary of State Dulles stated that he did not "expect that there is going to be a Communist victory in Indochina"; that "in terms of Communist domination of Indochina, I do not accept that as a probability." . . .

Despite this series of optimistic reports about eventual victory, every Member of the Senate knows that such victory today appears to be desperately remote, to say the least, despite tremendous amounts of economic and material aid from the United States, and despite a deplorable loss of French Union manpower. The call for either negotiations or additional participation by other nations underscores the remoteness of such a final victory today, regardless of the outcome at Dien Bien Phu. It is, of course, for these reasons that many French are reluctant to continue the struggle without greater assistance; for to record the sapping effect which time and the enemy have had on their will and strength in that area is not to disparage their valor....

Intervention in a War of Colonialism

I am frankly of the belief that no amount of American military assistance in Indochina can conquer an enemy which is everywhere and at the same time nowhere, "an enemy of the people" which has the sympathy and covert support of the people. As succinctly stated by the report of the Judd Subcommittee of the House Foreign Affairs Committee in January of this year:

> Until political independence has been achieved, an effective fighting force from the associated states cannot be expected.... The apathy of the local population to the menace of Viet Minh communism disguised as nationalism is the most discouraging aspect of the situation. That can only be overcome through the grant of complete independence to each of the associated states. Only for such a cause as their own freedom will people make the most heroic effort necessary to win this kind of struggle.

This is an analysis which is shared, if in some instances grudgingly, by most American observers. Moreover, without political independence for the associated states, the other Asiatic nations have made it clear that they regard this as a war of colonialism; and the "united action" which is said to be so desperately needed for victory in that area is likely to end up as unilateral action by our own country. Such intervention, without participation by the armed forces of the other nations of Asia, without the support of the great masses of the peoples of the associated states, with increasing reluctance and discouragement on the part of the French—and, I might add, with hordes of Chinese Communist troops poised just across the border in anticipation of our unilateral entry into their kind of battleground—such intervention, Mr. President, would be virtually impossible in the type of military situation which prevails in Indochina.

"It is preposterous to maintain that we should reduce our effort and lessen our commitment to the great struggle of our century."

The US Must Maintain Its Commitments (1965)

Thomas J. Dodd

Thomas J. Dodd was a Democratic Senator from Connecticut and a supporter of President Lyndon B. Johnson's Vietnam policy. The following viewpoint is excerpted from a speech he delivered to the US Senate in 1965. In it, Mr. Dodd describes the dangers of "the new isolationism" and states his belief that the United States must maintain its long-time stance of aiding people who are trying to defend or maintain liberty.

As you read, consider the following questions:

1. How does Mr. Dodd define "the new isolationism"? Why does he see this view as being "potentially disastrous"?
2. According to Mr. Dodd, why would it have been wrong for the US to withdraw from Vietnam?
3. What is "the disease, the epidemic" that Mr. Dodd says we were resisting in Vietnam? What were its dangers, in his view?

Thomas J. Dodd, speech to the US Senate, February 23, 1965.

There has been developing in this country in recent years a brand of thinking about foreign affairs which, I believe, can aptly be described as "the new isolationism." This internal phenomenon is, in my opinion, potentially more disastrous in terms of its consequence than the major external problems that confront us.

Its background is a growing national weariness with Cold War burdens we have been so long carrying, a rising frustration with situations that are going against us in many places, a long-simmering indignation over the fact that our generosity and sacrifice have too often been met abroad, not just with indifference and ingratitude, but even with hostility and contempt.

Its political base seems to be to the Left of center, although it forms as yet a distinct minority there.

Its scareword is "escalation"; its cure-all is "neutralization."

Its prophets include some of my colleagues in the Congress, influential spokesmen in the press, and leading figures in the academic world. Some are new volunteers in this cause of retrenchment; they regard themselves as pragmatists. Others are old hands at Pollyanna-ism, those unshakable romantics who were disillusioned by Moscow at the time of the Hitler-Stalin pact, disillusioned by Mao when they discovered that he was not really an agrarian reformer, disillusioned by Castro when they learned he was not a cross between Thomas Jefferson and Robin Hood—and who, having again dusted themselves off, now look for new vistas of adventure....

New Isolationism

The basic premise of the new isolationism is that the United States is overextended in its attempt to resist Communist aggression around the world, overcommitted to the defense of distant outposts, and overinvolved in the murky and unintelligible affairs of remote areas.

The corollaries of the new isolationism are many. It is contended that we should de-emphasize the Cold War and reverse our national priorities in favor of domestic improvements; that we should withdraw from South Viet-Nam; that we should cease involvement in the Congo; that we should relax the so-called rigidity of our Berlin policy; that foreign aid has outlived its usefulness and should be severely cut back; that our Military Establishment and our C.I.A. organizations that seem particularly suspect because they are symbols of world-wide involvement, should be humbled and "cut down to size" and stripped of their influence in foreign policy questions.

In my judgment all of these propositions have one thing in common. Each of them would strike at the heart of our national effort to preserve our freedom and our security; and collectively they add up to a policy which I can describe by no other name than "appeasement," subtle appeasement, unintentional appeasement, to be sure, but appeasement nonetheless.

My purpose this afternoon then, is to oppose these propositions and to enlist Senators' opposition against them—for the new isolationism is as bankrupt as the old.

US Not Overextended

First of all—to tackle the main premise—I reject the assumption that the United States is overextended, or overcommitted, or overinvolved.

We are enjoying a spectacular growth in every index of national strength. Our population, our wealth, our industrial capacity, our scientific potential, our agricultural output, all are enjoying great upward surges. We were informed that our Gross National Product was again up in January, and the trend seems ever upward.

Commitment of Honor

I want to say that these advocates of retreat, defeat, surrender, and national dishonor have not been doing the country any good when they went before a television network suggesting that this Nation was not committed to fighting aggression in this area. The Senate voted for the resolution last year, and Senators voted that this country would help that country resist aggression, and specifically authorized the President to take whatever steps he felt necessary to resist further aggression. We are committed. We have more than 200,000 men there. We have at stake our national honor. We are committed to resisting Communist aggression. That is what this is all about.

Russell Long, *Congressional Record*, February 16, 1966.

Far from overextending ourselves in the Cold War, we are actually in a period of declining defense budgets, of steadily lowered draft calls, of sharply reduced foreign aid, of one tax cut after another.

Let me emphasize this: In every basic resource, we have greater capacity today than during the past five years; by every military or economic standard, we are stronger; and by every physical measurement, the percentage of our resources going into the Cold War is lower. Why then should we talk of weariness or overcommitment?

We are not even straining ourselves. We are actually pursuing today a policy not only of both guns and butter, but of less guns and more butter.

So far as our resources go, we are capable of indefinite continuation and even intensification of our present efforts, if need be. It is only our mental, and perhaps our moral, resources which seem to be feeling the strain.

We would, of course, prefer to live in a world in which it were possible for us to have no commitments, a world in which we could devote all of our energies to the task of perfecting our society at home and enriching the lives of our people.

War of Survival

But we must face the world as it is. And the basic fact of our world is that Western civilization, itself terribly rent and divided, both politically and philosophically, has been forced into a twilight war of survival by a relentless and remorseless enemy.

It is incontestable, in terms of people enslaved and nations gobbled up over the past twenty years, that we have not been holding our own. And each year, the world Communist movement is committing more and more of its resources to the task of subjugating our allies, all around the perimeter of freedom.

Against this background it is preposterous to maintain that we should reduce our effort and lessen our commitment to the great struggle of our century.

Yet, according to *Time* magazine, it is the wide-spread sentiment of the academic world that we have overreached ourselves and ought to pull back. Walter Lippmann, the well-known columnist, for whom I have great respect, says that "the American tide will have to recede."

It has been argued that we would be in a "precarious situation" if we were attacked on several fronts. Of course we would, but does anyone believe that we can solve the problem by abandoning our commitments and defensive alliances? Would the loss of these countries be any the less disastrous because they were given up undefended?

On the contrary, if we are not strong enough to honor our commitments today, then we should solve the problem, not by reducing our commitments, but by becoming stronger, and by aiding our allies to become stronger.

Delicate Balance

The defense of the free world rests on a very delicate balance. The key elements in that balance are American power and American determination. If we lack the power to maintain that balance, then certainly all is lost. If we reveal that we lack the determination, if we, for instance, allow ourselves to be pushed out of Viet-Nam, such a humiliation may indeed be the second shot heard around the world; and a dozen nations might soon throw in the sponge and make whatever accommodation they could with an enemy that would then seem assured of victory.

Four years ago, after a visit to Southeast Asia, I said on the floor of the Senate:

If the United States, with its unrivaled might, with its unparalleled wealth, with its dominion over sea and air, with its heritage as the champion of freedom—if this United States and its free-world allies have so diminished in spirit that they can be laid in the dust by a few thousand primitive guerrillas, then we are far down the road from which there is no return.

In right and in might, we are able to work our will on this question. Southeast Asia cannot be lost unless we will it to be lost; it cannot be saved unless we will it to be saved.

This problem, seemingly so remote and distant, will in fact be resolved here in the United States, in the Congress, in the administration, and in the minds and hearts of the American people.

The passage of four years has not diminished my belief in this course....

Responsible Support

No responsible world leader suggests that we should withdraw our support from Vietnam. To do so would unhinge a vast and vital area, thereby committing to Communist domination its resources and its people. This we cannot do. Therefore, we need the dedication and the courage to face some hard and unpleasant facts. We are at war in Vietnam and we must have the will to win that war. . . .

This nation must back up its resolve with whatever manpower, equipment, and weaponry it may take, first to stem the Communist advance in Laos and Vietnam, and then to help these countries, along with their neighbors in Thailand, to create conditions of stability and freedom in Southeast Asia. The security of all Asia hinges on this crucial battle.

Barry Goldwater, *Where I Stand*, 1964.

Twenty-five years ago, our country, comparatively new and untried among the great nations of the earth, through passage of the Lend-Lease Act, described by Winston Churchill as "the most unsordid act of recorded history," embarked irrevocably upon the path that has brought us to our present posture in history. Through that act, we affirmed the preservation and expansion of liberty as our highest goal; we acknowledged that freedom was insecure everywhere so long as tyranny existed anywhere; and we assumed the burden, and the glory, of being the champion and defender of man's highest aspirations.

Since that embattled hour, when the light of freedom was but a flicker in the dark, our journey across the pages of history has been fantastic and unprecedented: tragic, to be sure, in its mistakes and naiveties, but heroic in its innovations and commitments, prodigious in its energy and power, gigantic in its generosity and good will, noble in its restraint and patience, and sublime in its purpose and in its historic role.

We have not realized the high goals we set for ourselves in World War II.

But we have preserved freedom and national independence in more than half the earth; we have prevented the nuclear holocaust; we have restored Western Europe; we have helped friend and foe to achieve prosperity, freedom and stability; we have launched a world-peace organization and have kept it alive; we have offered the hand of friendship and help to the impoverished and backward peoples of the world if they will but take it.

Irresponsible Isolationism

It may be said of our country today, as of no other in history, that wherever people are willing to stand up in defense of their liberty, Americans stand with them.

We cannot know at this hour whether our journey has just begun or is nearing its climax; whether the task ahead is the work of a generation, or of a century. President Kennedy said, in his Inaugural Address, that the conflict would not be resolved in our lifetime.

The Chief of Staff of the Army recently told the Congress that it might well take ten years to decide the issue in Viet-Nam alone. And Viet-Nam is only one symptom of the disease, the epidemic, we are resisting.

Against this somber background, how foolish it is to talk of de-emphasizing the Cold War, of pulling out of Viet-Nam, of abandoning the Congo to Communist intrigue, of slashing the defense budget by 10 per cent, or of any of the other irresponsibilities of the new isolationism.

"The true fact is that the United States has had no obligation to South Viet-Nam or anyone else under the SEATO treaty to use its own armed forces in the defense of South Viet-Nam."

The US Has No Binding Commitments (1965)

Don R. Larson and Arthur Larson

Don R. Larson was Director of the US Information Agency under President Eisenhower. Arthur Larson was a professor of political science who served as the first head of the Department of Public Administration at the University of Punjab, Lahore, West Pakistan. In the following viewpoint the authors state that ideas of America's commitments in Southeast Asia are based on false interpretations of treaties and agreements the US has made in the past.

As you read, consider the following questions:

1. According to the authors, on what two documents was the United States' "Commitment" to South Viet-Nam based?
2. How much actual commitment do they say these documents give us?
3. What do the Larsons say is our "one obligation"?

Don R. Larson and Arthur Larson, from *Vietnam and Beyond*, Rule of Law Research Center, Duke University, 1965. Reprinted with permission of Arthur Larson.

The point of no return is rapidly being approached in Viet-Nam. The Marines have landed. Our planes and our men are engaged in almost daily bombing of a foreign land and people. The sending of ground forces in division strength is hinted at by the Army Chief of Staff. The committing of as many as 250,000 American troops is in the short-range contingency planning. The prospect of thousands of American men laying down their lives in a war on the Asiatic mainland looms larger with every day that passes.

Why?

Every time President Johnson is asked this question—and he now says that he has answered it over fifty times—the first reason he gives is always the same: We must do what we are doing to honor the commitments we have made to the Vietnamese people ever since 1954.

President Johnson bases his statement on two documents: the letter of President Eisenhower to President Diem of October 23, 1954, and the Southeast Asia Collective Defense treaty and protocol ratified in February 1955.

Eisenhower Letter

To understand the purpose of the Eisenhower letter, one must recall that it followed directly upon an agreement with France that "economic aid, budgetary support, and other assistance" would thereafter be furnished directly to Laos, to Viet-Nam, and Cambodia, rather than through France. Pursuant to this understanding, President Eisenhower wrote to President Diem to open discussion of this possibility. After a brief introduction and reference to our aid with the refugee problem, he said:

> We have been exploring ways and means to permit our aid to Viet-Nam to be more effective and to make a greater contribution to the welfare and stability of the Government of Viet-Nam. I am, accordingly, instructing the American Ambassador to Viet-Nam to examine with you in your capacity as Chief of Government, how an intelligent program of American aid given directly to your Government, can serve to assist Viet-Nam in its present hour of trial, provided that your Government is prepared to give assurances as to the standards of performance it would be able to maintain in the event such aid were supplied.
>
> The purpose of this offer is to assist the Government of Viet-Nam in developing and maintaining a strong, viable state, capable of resisting attempted subversion or aggression through military means. The Government of the United States expects that this aid will be met by performance on the part of the Government of Viet-Nam in undertaking needed reforms. It hopes that such aid, combined with your own continuing efforts, will contribute effectively toward an independent Viet-Nam endowed with a strong government. Such a government would, I hope, be so responsive to the nationalist aspirations of its people, so enlightened in purpose and effective in performance, and it

will be respected both at home and abroad and discourage anyone who might wish to impose a foreign ideology on your free people.

That is all....

No Pledge of Commitment

Where in this highly tentative, highly conditional opening of negotiations and statement of hopes is the "commitment," the "obligation," the pledging of our word? Even if we seem to have indicated a willingness to do something to help, what is that something—beyond aid in developing a strong, viable state?

The actual assistance program during the Eisenhower Administration confirms this concept. Of total aid from 1953 to 1961, less than one-fourth was classified as military, and more than three-fourths economic. Some idea of the relatively small size of the military side may be seen from the announcement on May 5, 1960, that the Military Assistance and Advisory Group would be increased by the end of the year from 327 to 685.

In short, the nearest thing to a commitment at this stage was an indicated willingness, subject to some stiff (and as yet unsatisfied) conditions and understandings, to provide economic and technical assistance, including military advisers, material, and training.

The other document allegedly imposing an obligation on us to fight to defend South Viet-Nam is a legal instrument, the SEATO treaty, signed in September, 1954, and ratified in February, 1955....

The true fact is that the United States has had no obligation to South Viet-Nam or anyone else under the SEATO treaty to use its own armed forces in the defense of South Viet-Nam....

The 'Containment' Policy in Asia

Reprinted with permission from the Minneapolis Star and Tribune.

The specified events calling for direct action have not occurred.
The two operative defense provisions of the SEATO treaty occur in Article IV. They are set in motion by two different kinds of events, and call for two entirely different kinds of action by the parties.

Paragraph 1 comes into play when there is "aggression by armed attack." The obligation on each party is "to meet the common danger in accordance with its constitutional processes."

Paragraph 2 applies when "the territory or the sovereignty or political independence of any (covered area)...is threatened in any way other than by armed attack or is affected or threatened by any fact or situation which might endanger the peace of the area." In this event, the only obligation is that "the Parties shall consult immediately in order to agree on the measures which should be taken for the common defense."...

If the first type of "overt military aggression" occurred, [Secretary of State John Foster] Dulles said:

> The United States would of course invoke the processes of the United Nations and consult with its allies. But we could not escape ultimate responsibility for decisions closely touching our own security and self-defense.

But as to the second type of situation he said:

> The situation in Indochina is not that of open military aggression by the Chinese Communist regime. Thus, in Indochina, the problem is one of restoring tranquility in an area where disturbances are fomented from Communist China, but where there is not open invasion from Communist China.

Task of Pacification

And now note the pointblank statement of how *not* to deal with this problem:

> This task of pacification, in our opinion, cannot be successfully met merely by unilateral armed intervention.

Which is precisely what we are attempting today.

He goes on to say:

> Some other conditions need to be established. Throughout these Indochina developments, the United States has held to a stable and consistent course and has made clear the conditions which, in its opinion, might justify intervention. These conditions were and are (1) an invitation from the present lawful authorities; (2) clear assurance of complete independence to Laos, Cambodia, and Viet-Nam; (3) evidence of concern by the United Nations; (4) a joining in the collective effort of some of the other nations in the area; and (5) assurance that France will not itself withdraw from the battle until it is won.
>
> *Only if these conditions were realized could the President and the Congress be justified in asking the American people to make the sacrifices incident to commiting our Nation, with others, to using force to help to restore peace in the area.* (Italics supplied).

There, in plainest terms, was the real policy of the United States in 1954. It bears little resemblance to the present policy, which claims to have continued unchanged from that time to this.

Present policy ignores the peacekeeping role of the United Nations, tries to achieve pacification by unilateral armed intervention, and disregards all of Dulles' five conditions except the first, that of invitation—and there are even those who would disregard the first. Most conspicuously, there has been no significant joining in the collective effort by other nations of the area, and as for France staying in the battle until it is won—the less said about that the better.

Understanding Stereotypes

A **stereotype** is an oversimplified or exaggerated description. It can apply to things or people and be favorable or unfavorable. Quite often stereotyped beliefs about racial, religious, and national groups are insulting and oversimplified. They are usually based on misinformation or lack of information.

Part 1

Step 1.   The class should break into groups of four to six students. Each small group should examine the cartoon below, referring to the warming of US/China relations and the 1984 visit of President Reagan to China. After reflecting on the definition of a stereotype presented above, the members of each small group should discuss what stereotypes the cartoon suggests both the Americans and the Chinese may have applied to each other before their newly formed friendship. Each small group should choose a member to record the stereotypes it identifies.

Reprinted by permission of United Feature Syndicate.

Step 2. The small groups should next examine the following statements. Each individual, working separately, should mark the statements in the following fashion. *Mark S for any statement that is a stereotype. Mark NS for any statement that is not a stereotype. Mark U for statements for which determination is undecided or unsure.* Students should compare their rankings with others in their group, giving the reasons for their rankings.

> S = stereotype
> NS = not a stereotype
> U = undecided or unsure

1. Asian people are primitive and backward.
2. The Vietnamese do not value life as highly as most Americans.
3. The Japanese are masters at applying Western technology.
4. Asia consists of a wide range of landscapes and climatic regions.
5. Most Vietnamese are poor and not highly educated.
6. Vietnamese communism is evil.

7. Russian communism is evil.
8. Americans who fought in Vietnam were soldiers for freedom and democracy.

Step 3.   The small groups should next discuss the following questions:

1. Why does stereotyping exist?
2. What kind of situations tend to stereotype people?
3. Are stereotypes always harmful?
4. What harm can stereotyping cause?
5. What current stereotypes affect members of your small group?

Step 4.   Each small group should compare its results with other small groups in a classwide discussion.

"As South Vietnamese forces become stronger, the rate of American withdrawal can become greater."

Vietnamization Will Shorten the War (1969)

Richard M. Nixon

Richard M. Nixon was elected President of the United States in 1968 and 1972. He remained in that office until August 8, 1974 when he resigned under pressure resulting from his involvement in the cover-up of illegal activities during the 1972 political conventions. The following viewpoint is taken from a speech President Nixon delivered on national television at a time when the nation was in conflict. Mr. Nixon here explains why he believed that Vietnamization would enable the US to gradually withdraw its troops from Vietnam without the dire consequences of immediate withdrawal.

As you read, consider the following questions:

1. What does Mr. Nixon say is the main obstacle to peace?
2. What is "the Nixon doctrine"? "Vietnamization"?
3. Why did Mr. Nixon think that Vietnamization would be the only sound way to reduce US involvement in Vietnam?

Richard M. Nixon, speech delivered on national television, November 3, 1969.

Fifteen years ago North Vietnam, with the logistical support of Communist China and the Soviet Union, launched a campaign to impose a Communist government on South Vietnam by instigating and supporting a revolution.

In response to the request of the government of South Vietnam, President Eisenhower sent economic aid and military equipment to assist the people of South Vietnam in their efforts to prevent a Communist takeover. Seven years ago, President Kennedy sent 16,000 military personnel to Vietnam as combat advisors. Four years ago, President Johnson sent American combat forces to South Vietnam....

For these reasons, I rejected the recommendation that I should end the war by immediately withdrawing all our forces. I chose instead to change American policy on both the negotiating front and the battlefront....

Obstacle to Peace

It has become clear that the obstacle in negotiating an end to the war is not the President of the United States. And it is not the South Vietnamese.

The obstacle is the other side's absolute refusal to show the least willingness to join us in seeking a just peace. It will not do so while it is convinced that all it has to do is to wait for our next concession, and the next until it gets everything it wants.

There can now be no longer any question that progress in negotiation depends only on Hanoi's deciding to negotiate, to negotiate seriously.

I realize that this report on our efforts on the diplomatic fronts is discouraging to the American people, but the American people are entitled to know the truth—the bad news as well as the good news, where the lives of our young men are involved.

Now let me turn, however, to a more encouraging report on another front.

At the time we launched our search for peace I recognized we might not succeed in bringing an end to the war through negotiation. I, therefore, put into effect another plan to bring peace—a plan which will bring the war to an end regardless of what happens on the negotiating front.

The Nixon Doctrine

It is in line with a major shift in U.S. foreign policy which I described in my press conference at Guam on July 25. Let me briefly explain what has been described as the Nixon Doctrine—a policy which not only will help end the war in Vietnam, but which is an essential element of our program to prevent future Vietnams.

We Americans are a do-it-yourself-people. We are an impatient people. Instead of teaching someone else to do a job, we like to do

Richard M. Nixon

it ourselves. And this trait has been carried over into our foreign policy.

In Korea and again in Vietnam, the United States furnished most of the money, most of the arms, and most of the men to help the people of those countries defend their freedom against the Communist aggression.

Before any American troops were committed to Vietnam, a leader of another Asian country expressed this opinion to me when I was traveling in Asia as a private citizen. He said, "When you are trying to assist another nation defend its freedom, U.S. policy should be to help them fight the war but not to fight the war for them."

Well, in accordance with this wise counsel, I laid down in

Guam three principles as guidelines for future American policy toward Asia:

First, the United States will keep all of its treaty commitments.

Second, we shall provide a shield if a nuclear power threatens the freedom of a nation allied with us or of a nation whose survival we consider vital to our security.

Third, in cases involving other types of aggression, we shall furnish military and economic assistance when requested in accordance with our treaty commitments. But we shall look to the nation directly threatened to assume the primary responsibility of providing the manpower for its defense.

After I announced this policy, I found that the leaders of the Philippines, Thailand, Vietnam, South Korea, and other nations which might be threatened by Communist aggression, welcomed this new direction in American foreign policy.

Vietnamization

The defense of freedom is everybody's business—not just America's business. And it is particularly the responsibility of the people whose freedom is threatened. In the previous Administration, we Americanized the war in Vietnam. In this Administration, we are Vietnamizing the search for peace.

The policy of the previous Administration not only resulted in our assuming the primary responsibility for fighting the war but even more significantly did not adequately stress the goal of strengthening the South Vietnamese so that they could defend themselves when we left.

The Vietnamization Plan was launched following Secretary Laird's visit to Vietnam in March. Under the plan, I ordered first a substantial increase in the training and equipment of South Vietnamese forces.

In July, on my visit to Vietnam, I changed General Abrams' orders so that they were consistent with the objectives of our new policies. Under the new orders, the primary mission of our troops is to enable the South Vietnamese forces to assume the full responsibility for the security of South Vietnam.

Our air operations have been reduced by over 20 percent.

And now we have begun to see the results of this long overdue change in American policy in Vietnam.

Significant Results

After five years of Americans going into Vietnam, we are finally bringing American men home. By December 15, over 60,000 men will have been withdrawn from South Vietnam—including 20 percent of all of our combat forces.

The South Vietnamese have continued to gain in strength. As a result they have been able to take over combat responsibilities from our American troops.

Two other significant developments have occurred since this Administration took office.

Enemy infiltration, infiltration which is essential if they are to launch a major attack, over the last three months is less than 20 percent of what it was over the same period last year.

Most important—United States casualties have declined during the last two months to the lowest point in three years.

Honorable Peace

The operation has demonstrated that the Vietnamization program, designed to enable us to eventually remove our combat forces from South Vietnam, is progressing at an even more rapid rate than I had imagined. The operation has undoubtedly hastened the time when our objective of attaining an honorable peace can be achieved. . . .

I know that all Americans are tired of the war in Southeast Asia. I know the Congress and the administration is tired of the war. I am tired of the war. But I believe that most Americans would like to extricate ourselves in a manner which will encourage a stable peace. We should not leave a vacuum to be filled by Communists.

We must follow a responsible course. Vietnamization is such a course. I am convinced that the Cambodian operation has helped hasten Vietnamization and has helped to insure its success.

John Tower, *St. Paul Pioneer Press*, June 14, 1970.

Let me now turn to our program for the future.

We have adopted a plan which we have worked out in cooperation with the South Vietnamese for the complete withdrawal of all U.S. combat ground forces, and their replacement by South Vietnamese forces on an orderly scheduled timetable. This withdrawal will be made from strength and not from weakness. As South Vietnamese forces become stronger, the rate of American withdrawal can become greater.

No Timetable for Withdrawal

I have not and do not intend to announce the timetable for our program. There are obvious reasons for this decision which I am sure you will understand. As I have indicated on several occasions, the rate of withdrawal will depend on developments on three fronts.

One of these is the progress which can be or might be made in the Paris talks. An announcement of a fixed timetable for our withdrawal would completely remove any incentive for the enemy to negotiate an agreement.

They would simply wait until our forces had withdrawn and then move in.

The other two factors on which we will base our withdrawal decisions are the level of enemy activity and the progress of the training program of the South Vietnamese forces. I am glad to be able to report tonight progress on both of these fronts has been greater than we anticipated when we started the program in June for withdrawal. As a result, our timetable for withdrawal is more optimistic now than when we made our first estimates in June. This clearly demonstrates why it is not wise to be frozen in on a fixed timetable.

We must retain the flexibility to base each withdrawal decision on the situation as it is at that time rather than on estimates that are no longer valid.

Along with this optimistic estimate, I must—in all candor—leave one note of caution.

If the level of enemy activity significantly increases we might have to adjust our timetable accordingly.

No Misunderstandings

However, I want the record to be completely clear on one point.

At the time of the bombing halt just a year ago, there was some confusion as to whether there was an understanding on the part of the enemy that if we stopped the bombing of North Vietnam they would stop the shelling of cities in South Vietnam. I want to be sure that there is no misunderstanding on the part of the enemy with regard to our withdrawal program.

We have noted the reduced level of infiltration, the reduction of our casualties, and are basing our withdrawal decisions partially on those factors.

If the level of infiltration or our casualties increase while we are trying to scale down the fighting, it will be the result of a conscious decision by the enemy.

Hanoi could make no greater mistake than to assume that an increase in violence will be to its advantage. If I conclude that increased enemy action jeopardizes our remaining forces in Vietnam, I shall not hesitate to take strong and effective measures to deal with that situation.

This is not a threat. This is a statement of policy which as Commander-in-Chief of our Armed Forces I am making in meeting my responsibility for the protection of American fighting men wherever they may be.

Only Two Choices

My fellow Americans, I am sure you recognize from what I have said that we really only have two choices open to us if we want to end this war.

I can order an immediate, precipitate withdrawal of all Americans from Vietnam without regard to the effects of that action.

Or we can persist in our search for a just peace through a negotiated settlement if possible, or through continued implementation of our plan for Vietnamization if necessary—a plan in which we will withdraw all of our forces from Vietnam on a schedule in accordance with our program, as the South Vietnamese become strong enough to defend their own freedom.

I have chosen the second course.

It is not the easy way.

It is the right way.

It is a plan which will end the war and serve the cause of peace—not just in Vietnam but in the Pacific and in the world.

Supporting Vietnamization

Vietnamization of the war. This is the policy adopted by my government, which I support, under present conditions.

When I was the commander of Korea, I visited the French then fighting in Vietnam. I urged them to start a training program for the South Vietnamese, similar to the successful one we were using for Koreans. This was not accepted.

The best way for the United States to extricate itself from Vietnam with honor is to train the South Vietnam army and to equip it with modern weapons.

As these troops assume responsibilities which are now ours, our soldiers should be brought home as the military situation permits, remembering that we still have 50,000 troops in Korea 17 years after the armistice.

General Mark W. Clark, *New York Times*, 1970.

In speaking of the consequences of a precipitate withdrawal, I mentioned that our allies would lose confidence in America.

Far more dangerous, we would lose confidence in ourselves. The immediate reaction would be a sense of relief that our men were coming home. But as we saw the consequences of what we had done, inevitable remorse and divisive recrimination would scar our spirit as a people.

We have faced other crises in our history and have become stronger by rejecting the easy way out and taking the right way in meeting our challenges. Our greatness as a nation has been our capacity to do what had to be done when we knew our course was right.

"The Vietnamization policy is based on the same false premises which have doomed to failure our previous military efforts in Vietnam."

Vietnamization Will Extend the War (1970)

George S. McGovern

George S. McGovern, one of the first Congressional critics of American military intervention in South Vietnam, is a former Democratic senator from South Dakota. In 1972 he ran for President but was defeated by Richard M. Nixon. The following viewpoint is taken from a statement he made during hearings before the Senate Committee on Foreign Relations. In it he criticizes Vietnamization of the war and suggests that instead the US should support Vietnamization of the Vietnamese government.

As you read, consider the following questions:

1. Why does Mr. McGovern believe that the US government should stop supporting the Thieu-Ky regime?
2. Why does he believe that Vietnamization cannot work as a means of disengaging the US from Vietnam?
3. What does he mean when he says that the US should encourage the Vietnamization of the government?

George S. McGovern, statement before US Senate Committee on Foreign Relations, February 4, 1970.

Mr. Chairman, and members of the committee, the resolution that I have submitted with the cosponsorship of Senators Church, Cranston, Goodell, Hughes, McCarthy, Moss, Nelson, Ribicoff, and Young of Ohio calls for the withdrawal from Vietnam of all U.S. forces, the pace to be limited only by these three considerations: the safety of our troops during the withdrawal process, the mutual release of prisoners of war, and arrangements for asylum in friendly countries for any Vietnamese who might feel endangered by our disengagement. (I have recently been advised by the Department of Defense that the 484,000 men we now have in Vietnam could be transported to the United States at a total cost of $144,519,621.)

This process of orderly withdrawal could be completed, I believe, in less than a year's time.

Such a policy of purposeful disengagement is the only appropriate response to the blunt truth that there will be no resolution of the war so long as we cling to the Thieu-Ky regime. That government has no dependable political base other than the American military presence and it will never be accepted either by its challengers in South Vietnam or in Hanoi.

We can continue to pour our blood and substance into a neverending effort to support the Saigon hierarchy or we can have peace, but we cannot have both General Thieu and an end to the war.

Barrier to Peace and Healing

Our continued military embrace of the Saigon regime is the major barrier, both to peace in Southeast Asia and to the healing of our society. It assures that the South Vietnamese generals will take no action to build a truly representative government which can either compete with the NLF or negotiate a settlement of the war. It deadlocks the Paris negotiations and prevents the scheduling of serious discussions on the release and exchange of prisoners of war. It diverts our energies from critical domestic needs. It sends young Americans to be maimed or killed in a war that we cannot win and that will not end so long as our forces are there in support of General Thieu.

I have long believed that there can be no settlement of the Vietnam struggle until some kind of provisional coalition government assumes control in Saigon. But this is precisely what General Thieu will never consider. After the Midway conference last June he said, "I solemnly declare that there will be no coalition government, no peace cabinet, no transitional government, not even a reconciliatory government."

Although President Nixon has placed General Thieu as one of the two or three greatest statesmen of our age, Thieu has brushed off the suggestion that he broaden his government and has denounced those who advocate or suggest a negotiated peace as pro-Communist racketeers and traitors. A coalition government means death, he has said.

Prescription for Endless War

Mr. Chairman, let us not delude ourselves. This is a clear prescription for an endless war, and changing its name to Vietnamization still leaves us tied to a regime that cannot successfully wage war or make peace.

When administration officials expressed the view that American combat forces might be out of Vietnam by the end of 1970, General Thieu called a press conference last month and insisted that this was an "impossible and impractical goal" and that instead withdrawal "will take many years."

And yet there is wide currency to the view that America's course in Southeast Asia is no longer an issue, that the policy of Vietnamization promises an early end of hostilities. That is a false hope emphatically contradicted not only by our ally in Saigon but by the tragic lessons of the past decade.

Tragic Hoax

"Vietnamization" has now been fully revealed for a tragic hoax. . . .

It is now clear that the President has not abandoned the disastrous objective of the last tragic decade. It is *military victory* that he seeks— the perpetuation of whatever anticommunist government can be found,—however corrupt, unpopular, or undemocratic, and however little they will fight to defend themselves, by whatever military means are necessary. It is a policy which seeks to preserve an American bridgehead on the Mainland of Southeast Asia. . . .

We cannot have it both ways. We cannot have both disengagement and escalation. We cannot hold to a goal of peace, disengagement, and a "political solution" while expanding the war and seeking the total destruction of the enemy.

Walter F. Mondale, speech, May 19, 1970.

As I understand the proposal, Vietnamization directs the withdrawal of American troops only as the Saigon armed forces demonstrate their ability to take over the war. Yet a preponderance of evidence indicates that the Vietnamese people do not feel the Saigon regime is worth fighting for. Without local support, "Vietnamization" becomes a plan for the permanent deployment of American combat troops, and not a strategy for disengagement. The President has created a fourth branch of the American Government by giving Saigon a veto over American foreign policy.

If we follow our present policy in Vietnam, there will still be an American Army in my opinion, of 250,000 or 300,000 men in Southeast Asia 15 or 20 years hence or perhaps indefinitely. Meanwhile American firepower and bombardment will have killed more tens of thousands of Vietnamese who want nothing other than an end of the war. All this to save a corrupt, unrepresentative regime in Saigon.

Any military escalation by Hanoi or the Vietcong would pose a challenge to American forces which would require heavier American military action and, therefore, heavier American casualties, or we would be faced with the possibility of a costly, forced withdrawal.

False Premises for Vietnamization

The Vietnamization policy is based on the same false premises which have doomed to failure our previous military efforts in Vietnam. It assumes that the Thieu-Ky regime in Saigon stands for freedom and a popularly backed regime. Actually, the Saigon regime is an oppressive dictatorship which jails its critics and blocks the development of a broadly based government. Last June 20, the Saigon minister for liaison for parliament, Von Huu Thu, confirmed that 34,540 political prisoners were being held and that many of those people were non-Communists who were guilty of nothing more than advocating a neutral peaceful future for their country. In proportion to population the political prisoners held by Saigon would be the equivalent of a half million political prisoners in the United States.

The Thieu-Ky regime is no closer to American ideals than its challenger, the National Liberation Front. Indeed self-determination and independence are probably far stronger among the Vietnamese guerrillas and their supporters than within the Saigon Government camp.

I have never felt that American interests and ideals were represented by the Saigon generals or their corrupt predecessors. We should cease our embrace of this regime now and cease telling the American people that it stands for freedom.

I should like to make clear that I am opposed to both the principle and the practice of the policy of Vietnamization. I am opposed to the policy, whether it works by the standard of its proponents or does not work. I oppose as immoral and self-defeating a policy which gives either American arms or American blood to perpetuate a corrupt and unrepresentative foreign regime. It is not in the interests of either the American or the Vietnamese people to maintain such a government.

I find it morally and politically repugnant for us to create a client group of Vietnamese generals in Saigon and then give them murderous military technology to turn against their own people.

George S. McGovern

Vietnamization is basically an effort to tranquilize the conscience of the American people while our Government wages a cruel and needless war by proxy.

An enlightened American foreign policy would cease trying to dictate the outcome of an essentially local struggle involving various groups of Vietnamese. If we are concerned about a future threat to Southeast Asia from China, let us have the common sense to recognize that a strong independent regime even though organized by the National Liberation Front and Hanoi would provide a more dependable barrier to Chinese imperialism than the weak puppet regime we have kept in power at the cost of 40,000 American lives and hundreds of thousands of Vietnamese lives.

Even if we could remove most of our forces from Vietnam, how could we justify before God and man the use of our massive firepower to continue a slaughter that neither serves our interests nor the interests of the Vietnamese.

The policy of Vietnamization is a cruel hoax designed to screen from the American people the bankruptcy of a needless military involvement in the affairs of the Vietnamese people. Instead of Vietnamizing the war let us encourage the Vietnamization of the government in South Vietnam. We can do that by removing the embrace that now prevents other political groups from assuming a leadership role in Saigon, groups that are capable of expressing the desire for peace of the Vietnamese people.

Recognizing Ethnocentric Statements

Ethnocentrism is the attitude or tendency of people to view their race, religion, culture, group, or nation as superior to others, and to judge others on that basis. An American whose custom is to eat with a fork or spoon would be making an ethnocentric statement when saying, "The Vietnamese custom of eating with chopsticks is stupid."

Ethnocentrism has promoted much misunderstanding and conflict. It emphasizes cultural and religious differences and the notion that one's national institutions or group customs are superior.

Ethnocentrism limits people's ability to be objective and to learn from others. Education in the truest sense stresses the similarities of the human condition throughout the world and the basic equality and dignity of all people.

Most of the following statements are taken from chapter one of this book. Some have other origins. Consider each statement carefully. *Mark E for any statement you think is ethnocentric. Mark NE for any statement you think is not ethnocentric. Mark U if you are undecided about any statement.*

If you are doing this activity as the member of a class or group, compare your answers with those of other class or group members. Be able to defend your answers. You may discover that others will come to different conclusions than you. Listening to the reasons others present for their answers may give you valuable insights in recognizing ethnocentric statements.

If you are reading this book alone, ask others if they agree with your answers. You too will find this interaction very valuable.

E = *ethnocentric*
NE = *not ethnocentric*
U = *undecided*

53

1. People of different cultures have many things in common.

2. Vietnam represents the cornerstone of the Free World in Southeast Asia.

3. God has marked America as a chosen nation.

4. Nations of the world must develop the ability to cooperate.

5. The Vietnamese are incapable of governing themselves without American help.

6. Americans are incapable of understanding the rich and complex culture of the Vietnamese.

7. Western civilization has been forced into a twilight war of survival by a relentless and remorseless enemy.

8. The defense of the Free World rests on a very delicate balance. The key elements in that balance are American power and American determination.

9. Wherever people are willing to stand up in defense of their liberty, Americans stand with them.

10. We Americans are a do-it-yourself people. We are an impatient people. Instead of teaching someone else to do a job, we like to do it ourselves.

11. Our greatness as a nation has been our capacity to do what had to be done when we knew the right course.

12. Chinese communism is superior to other brands of communism.

13. The Vietnamese people are unable to resist the advance of communism without US help.

14. The current American political system is more democratic than the current Vietnamese political system.

15. The United States is the only revolutionary nation which has truly maintained its ideals of freedom for all.

16. Many Americans believe that Communism and freedom cannot coexist.

Periodical Bibliography

The following list of periodical articles deals with the subject matter of this chapter.

Robert McAfee Brown — "US Cannot Act as the World's Policeman," *Christianity & Crisis,* May 23, 1975.

J.L. Collins — "What We're Doing in Vietnam," *U.S. News & World Report,* March 4, 1955.

John Foster Dulles — "The Goal of Our Foreign Policy," *Vital Speeches,* December 15, 1954.

Commonweal — "New Vietnam Commitment," February 23, 1962.

William H. Hunter — "A Way Toward Peace in Indochina," *The New Republic,* April 16, 1962.

Gilbert Jonas — "Southeast Asia: The Genesis of US Policy," *Vital Speeches,* April 15, 1962.

John F. Kennedy — "America's Stake in Vietnam," *Vital Speeches,* June 1, 1956.

Martin Luther King Jr. — Speech, April 4, 1967: "A Prophecy for the 80s," *Sojourners,* January 1983.

Joseph Kraft — "A Way Out in Viet-Nam," *Harper's,* December 1964.

Sidney Lens — "How It 'Really' All Began," *The Progressive,* June 1973.

Gale W. McGee — "Vietnam: A Living Example for Implementing the American Spirit," *Vital Speeches,* May 1, 1960.

R.P. Martin — "New Tactics or Endless War?" *U.S. News & World Report,* July 30, 1962.

Hans J. Morganthau — "The Realities of Containment," *The New Leader,* June 8, 1964.

Hans J. Morganthau — "Vietnam—Another Korea?" *Commentary,* May 1962.

Bill Moyers — "Vietnam: What Is Left to Conscience?" *Saturday Review,* February 13, 1971.

R.D. Murphy — "Guiding Principles in United States Foreign Policy," *Department of State Bulletin,* June 10, 1957.

The Nation — "Non-War and the Constitution," February 17, 1962.

Why Did US Policy Fail in Vietnam?

"The failure to declare war in Vietnam drove a wedge between the Army and large segments of the American public."

US Failure to Declare War Caused Defeat

Harry G. Summers Jr.

Colonel Harry G. Summers Jr., a former infantry battalion and corps operations officer in Vietnam, is currently on the staff of the Strategic Studies Institute of the Army War College at Carlisle, Pennsylvania. In 1980, wondering why the US "lost the war when it won all the battles," Colonel Summers began a study of US tactics and strategy in the Vietnam War. His conclusions point to strategic shortsightedness on the part of US policymakers. Foremost among US problems, in Colonel Summers' opinion, was the lack of a declaration of war which would have rallied the American public behind its military forces.

As you read, consider the following questions:

1. What reasons does the author suggest for President Johnson's failure to declare war against North Vietnam in 1964?
2. Why does Colonel Summers think the failure to declare war put the Army into a "dangerous position"?
3. What does William F. Buckley claim is an important result of declaring war?

Reprinted with permission from *On Strategy: A Critical Analysis of the Vietnam War* by Harry G. Summers Jr. Published 1982 by Presidio Press, 31 Pamaron Way, Novato, California.

One of the continuing arguments about the Vietnam war is whether or not a formal declaration of war would have made any difference. On the one hand there are those who see a declaration of war as a kind of magic talisman that would have eliminated all of our difficulties. On the other hand there are those who see a declaration of war as a clear statement of *initial* public support which focuses the nation's attention on the enemy. (Continuation of this initial public support is, of course, contingent on the successful prosecution of war aims.) As we will see, it was the lack of such focus on the enemy and on the political objectives to be obtained by the use of military force that was the crux of our strategic failure.

A Declaration of War

Further, a...declaration of war makes the prosecution of the war a shared responsibility of both the government and the American people. Without a declaration of war the Army was caught on the horns of a dilemma. It was ordered into battle by the Commander-In-Chief, the duly elected President of the United States. It was sustained in battle by appropriations by the Congress, the elected representatives of the American people. The legality of its commitment was not challenged by the Supreme Court of the United States. Yet, because there was no formal declaration of war, many vocal and influential members of the American public questioned (and continue to question) the legality and propriety of its actions....

The requirement for a declaration of war was rooted in the principle of civilian control of the military, and the failure to declare war in Vietnam drove a wedge between the Army and large segments of the American public.

It is not as if we did not know better. We knew perfectly well the importance of maintaining the bond between the American people and their soldiers in the field, and that this bond was the source of our moral strength....

President Johnson could probably have had a declaration of war in August 1964 after the Gulf of Tonkin incidents when two American destroyers were attacked by North Vietnamese patrol boats. Instead of asking for a declaration of war, however, President Johnson asked Congress for a resolution empowering him to "take all necessary measures to repel an armed attack against the forces of the United States and to prevent further aggression." This Southeast Asia Resolution (better known as the Gulf of Tonkin resolution) passed the Senate by a vote of 88-2, and the House by a unanimous voice vote of 416-0....

When the President could have had it he didn't think he needed it, and when he needed it he couldn't have it. As the distinguished historian Arthur M. Schlesinger, Jr. commented, "[President]

WIELDING THE BIG STICK

LACK OF
NATIONAL
RESOLVE

U.S.
FOREIGN
POLICY

Distributed by L.A. Times Syndicate

Johnson could certainly have obtained congressional authoriza-
tion beyond the Tonkin Gulf resolution for a limited war in Vietnam in 1965. He might even, had he wished (but no one wished),
have obtained a declaration of war." The reason why neither the
President nor the Congress (nor the military either, for that mat-

ter) seemed to think a declaration of war was necessary, and why the President deliberately did not seek to mobilize public support for such a proposal was that initially no one envisioned a 10-year war, the massive commitment of American ground troops, nor the ground swell of American opposition. It was hoped that the use of US tactical air power in South Vietnam, the "Rolling Thunder" air campaign against North Vietnam and the limited use of US troops to protect air bases and logistics installations would cause the North Vietnamese to halt their aggression.

Why Not Declare War?

By the spring of 1965 it was obvious that such a limited response was not effective, and the decision was made to commit US ground combat troops to the war. Rather than go back to the Congress and ask for a declaration of war, writes Herbert Y. Schandler in *The Unmaking of a President: Lyndon Johnson and Vietnam,* "efforts were made to make the change as imperceptible as possible to the American public...." In retrospect this was a key strategic error. Failure to make this crucial political decision led to fear of making the political decision to mobilize the reserves. Failure to mobilize the reserves led to failure of the military leadership to push for strategic concepts aimed at halting North Vietnamese aggression and led to campaigns against the symptoms of the aggression—the insurgency in the South—rather than against the aggressor itself....For now we will limit our analysis to the question of why a declaration of war was not requested prior to the commitment of US ground combat forces.

One reason was that it would have seemed ludicrous for a great power like the United States to declare war on a tiny country like North Vietnam. War sanctions, both foreign and domestic, were deemed too massive to be appropriate. Another reason was the desire not to risk a Korea-style intervention by threatening Chinese security. There was also the danger that a formal declaration of war against North Vietnam might have triggered the implementation of security guarantees by China and the Soviet Union. Yet another reason may have been the fear that Congress would not approve such a declaration. This refusal would have caused an immediate halt to US efforts in South Vietnam (a preferable result, given the final outcome). A final reason may have been our use of the enemy's terminology to describe the nature of the war. In his analysis of our failure to declare war, University of California Professor Chalmers Johnson commented:

> [The label "People's War"] made it harder for a counterinsurgent state, such as the United States, to clarify for its own citizens exactly whom it was fighting when it defended against a people's war. Steeped in the legalistic concept that wars are between states, the American public became confused by its

government's failure to declare war on North Vietnam and thereby identify the *state* with which the United States was at war.... .

Presidential Authority

Instead of seeking further congressional support for the war, President Johnson took the opposite tack and fell back on his authority as President. In March 1966, the Legal Advisor to the Department of State told the Senate Committee on Foreign Relations:

> There can be no question in present circumstances of the President's authority to commit US forces to the defense of South Vietnam. The grant of authority to the President in article II of the Constitution extends to the actions of the United States currently undertaken in Vietnam.

Emphasizing this point in a news conference on 18 August 1967, President Johnson said, "We stated then, and we repeat now, we did not think the [Gulf of Tonkin] resolution was necessary to do what we did and what we're doing."

Presidential Error

President Johnson erred in relying on the Gulf of Tonkin resolution as his authority from the Congress to do what he deemed necessary in Southeast Asia. When dissent developed in 1966 and 1967, he would have been well advised to have gone back to the Congress for reaffirmation of the commitment to South Vietnam, a vote either of confidence or rejection. . . .President Johnson. . .should have forced the Congress to face its constitutional responsibility for waging war.

Harry G. Summers Jr., *On Strategy: A Critical Analysis of the Vietnam War*, 1982.

The only other time a declaration of war was politically feasible was when Richard M. Nixon assumed the Presidency in January 1969. He could have demanded that Congress either affirm our commitment with a declaration of war, giving him authority to prosecute the war to its conclusion, or reject the commitment, allowing him to immediately withdraw all American troops from Vietnam. But President Nixon had foreclosed this option with his campaign promises to bring the war to a close. Within weeks after assuming office, "Johnson's war" had become "Nixon's war." Like President Johnson, he fell back on his position as Commander-in-Chief as authority to prosecute the war.

Commenting on this, the Senate Committee on Foreign Relations said:

> The issue to be resolved is the proper locus within our con-

61

stitutional system of the authority to commit our country to war. More, perhaps, than ever before, the Executive and Congress are in disagreement as to where that authority properly lies. It is the Executive's view, manifested in both words and action, that the President, in his capacity as Commander in Chief, is properly empowered to commit the Armed Forces to hostilities in foreign countries. It is the committee's view—*conviction* may be the better word—that the authority to initiate war, as distinguished from acting to repel a sudden attack, is vested by the Constitution in the Congress and in the Congress alone....

Dangerous Position for Army

Into this so-called "legal vacuum" fell the US Army, caught in the middle between the executive and the legislative branches. This was a dangerous position for both the Army and for the Republic. It was dangerous for the Army because in failing to mobilize the national will the United States lost what Clausewitz called the strength of the passions of the American people strengthening and supporting us, the more vocal and passionate voices were too often raised in support of our enemies....

In the later stages, when the Vietnam war became a partisan political issue, the Army was placed in the untenable position of becoming involved in domestic politics solely because it was obeying its orders. As General Westmoreland observed:

> I recognized that it was not the job of the military to defend American commitment and policy. Yet it was difficult to differentiate between pursuit of a military task and such related matters as public and congressional support and the morale of the fighting man, who must be convinced that he is risking death for a worthy cause. The military thus was caught in between.

War Powers Act

This impasse continued as long as US troops were committed to Vietnam. It was not until November 1973 that Congress, over the President's veto, passed the War Powers Resolution in an attempt to increase congressional control. The purpose of the Resolution was:

> ...To fulfill the intent of the framers of the Constitution of the United States and insure that the collective judgment of both the Congress and the President will apply to the introduction of United States Armed Forces into hostilities, or into situations where imminent involvement in hostilities is clearly indicated by the circumstances, and to the continued use of such forces in hostilities or in such situations.

The Resolution requires the President to consult with the Congress before military forces are committed. Military involvement can continue for 60 days, and for another 30 days thereafter if the President certifies in writing that the safety of the force so requires. Unless Congress specifically authorizes it by a declaration of war, resolution or legislation, the involvement cannot be continued beyond the 90 days. As one observer noted:

> The law forces Congress to make a decision after two or at the most three months of confrontation. A vote to continue operations signifies the sharing of responsibility with the Executive; a vote to terminate signifies an assumption of responsibility by Congress alone.

Although the War Powers Resolution is a step toward solving the legal issues involved, it does not necessarily solve the moral and psychological issues so important to the Army. It raises the appalling specter of taking soldiers into combat and then being forced to disengage under fire because congressional approval was not forthcoming....

Effect of Declaration of War

We saw earlier that the congressional safeguard of a declaration of war had fallen out of fashion after World War II. But fashions change. Testifying before the Senate Foreign Relations Committee in March 1980 on the Iranian crisis, the distinguished scholar and diplomat George F. Kennan argued that the correct US response should have been a declaration of war. Not only would it have given the President clear-cut military authority, but it also would have provided nonmilitary options—e.g., internment of Iranian citizens, seizure of funds, US public concern would have been fixed and focused, and a clear signal would have been sent to the international community.

As columnist William F. Buckley observed:

> To declare war in this country would require a researcher to inform the President and Congress on just how to go about doing it. Declaring war is totally out of style. The post-Hiroshima assumption being that the declaration of war brings with it the tacit determination to use every weapon necessary in order to win that war. Thus we didn't go to war against North Korea, North Vietnam, or Cuba. But. . .
> To declare war is not necessarily to dispatch troops, let alone atom bombs. It is to recognize a juridically altered relationship and to license such action as is deemed appropriate. It is a wonderful demystifier . . . [leaving] your objective in very plain view.

One of the primary causes of our Vietnam failure was that we did not keep our "objective in very plain view." If a declaration of war could have accomplished that one task it could have been worth the effort.

"If the United States had not invested the situation in Vietnam with rivalry with Communist powers, the tragedy might have been avoided."

US Pride Caused Defeat

Walter H. Capps

Walter H. Capps, former director of the Robert Hutchins Center for the Study of Democratic Institutions, is professor of religious studies at the University of California, Santa Barbara. He has written and edited numerous books. In the following viewpoint Mr. Capps states that the United States, during the time of the Vietnamese conflict, was torn between two strong and conflicting views of the war. The view held by most policymakers saw Vietnam as a contest between the Superpowers. This view led to inappropriate aims and strategies and to defeat.

As you read, consider the following questions:

1. How does Mr. Capps define "the Armageddon mentality"? "the Eden mentality"?
2. According to the author, did the US become involved in Vietnam for selfish reasons? How did that change?
3. Why, according to Mr. Capps, was "the military adventure...confutable from the first"?

From *The Unfinished War: Vietnam and the American Conscience* by Walter H. Capps. Copyright © by Walter H. Capps. Reprinted by permission of Beacon Press.

The Vietnam War was fought in many places, on many fields, on many planes, all at the same time. The formal military activity was restricted to Indochina, but the war was also fought on television. Furthermore, it was waged on college and university campuses. One recalls the uprisings in Berkeley, the National Guard at Kent State, and the burning of the Bank of America building in Santa Barbara. On every campus, in every city square, and in virtually every living room a complex and multidimensional battle took place.

The conflict was enacted in less obvious ways too—not only in direct conflict, argumentation, protest marches, sit-ins, and rallies, but in changes in styles of art, music, and literature, and in shifts in modes of dress and manners. One could tell on which side of the issues people stood by the clothes they wore, the vocabulary they used, the literature they cited, the music they listened to, and of course the length and style they wore their hair.

Some said that the fundamental quarrel was not about the potential threat of communism in Vietnam, but about what it is to be an American, and indeed, what the future course of humankind ought to be.

Contrasting Cultures

As the events both at home and abroad, overt and subjective, worked their way, it became apparent that two contrasting American cultures had come into being. The differences in the ways each looked and thought became sharper than ethnic, racial, or economic distinctions. Two kinds of value systems had been spawned, with fissures deeper than those between Protestants and Catholics. Families were split, less by natural generational differences than by divergent attitudes, sensitivities, temperaments, and fundamental allegiances. The Biblical prophecy that when the great day comes, brothers will be turned against brothers, fathers against children, and children against parents seemed to have been fulfilled in the existing tensions. Each side complained that the other didn't understand what was happening. The other side responded that it couldn't understand because it couldn't hear.

Fundamentally, the Vietnam War was a contest between two views of human priorities [the Armageddon mentality and the Eden mentality]....

The world of Armageddon is shaped by conflict. The forces that prevail in life are the ones that win, that defeat their foes and demonstrate their superiority on the battlefield. Confrontations make allegiances firm, choices irreconcilable, and fidelities absolute. Events are always decisive, and the colossal drama toward which all things point is final. In Armageddon, the destiny of the world is enacted in struggles to the finish between diametrically

65

opposed power centers.

Eden resonates differently. Whatever boundaries pertain only differentiate Eden from all else; they have no internal bearing. Everything in Eden belongs; all inhabitants are citizens, and all are entitled to the resources of Eden, without exception. There are no hierarchies, no polarization, no stratification, no class struggle. There are no decisive choices, either; the goal is simply to maintain Eden. Eden is garden instead of battleground, it is harmony rather than conflict. It is warm, fecund, full of vegetation, beautiful, alluring, original, and all-encompassing. But Eden lacks precision.

The radical differences between the expectations of Armageddon and the impulses of Eden provide the framework for much of what has happened within the United States, and throughout the world, in the post-World War II era. Some of the time, for some of the people, motivation has come from Armageddon, while for others the compulsions have been those of Eden. The one encourages a readiness to confront the adversary; its temper is tough,

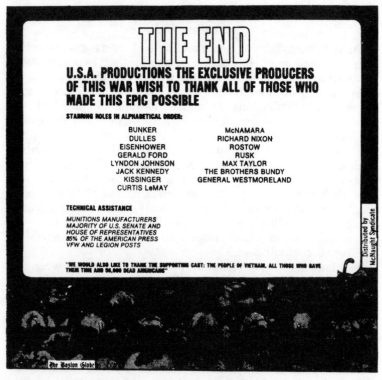

Reprinted with permission of the McNaught Syndicate, Inc.

resolute, defensive, self-protective. The other exhibits an interest in enunciating the underlying harmony; it speaks of maintaining the essential components of the living environment while proclaiming the blessings of global harmony....

For most of the post-World War II era, the inhabitants of Eden and the advocates of Armageddon have been at such severe odds that it has been as if there were two United States of America, competing with each other for supremacy and the allegiance of the citizenry....

Unresolved Quarrel

The trauma of Vietnam was a product of the projection of this fundamental quarrel onto the battlefield; what became most visible during the war was America in conflict with America—the dark night within the nation's soul. The war remains unfinished because the quarrel has not been resolved.

How did it happen this way? What forces gave the drama such orientation?

Dean Acheson, secretary of state under President Truman, offered some reminiscences that illuminate these questions. Writing in a book appropriately titled *Present at the Creation*, Acheson stated that it took some while for Americans to recognize that "the whole world structure and order that we had inherited from the nineteenth century was gone" after World War II. What replaced it, Acheson observed, was a struggle "directed from two bitterly opposed and ideologically irreconcilable power centers"—the world's great superpowers, whose rivalry had a pervasive influence upon all significant subsequent events.

Nearly thirty years later, Richard Nixon described the fundamental challenge in almost the same language that Acheson had used:

> The old colonial empires are gone. The new Soviet imperialism requires a new counterforce to keep it in check. The United States cannot provide this alone, but without strong and effective leadership from the United States, it cannot be provided at all. We cannot afford to waffle and waver. Either we act like a great power or we will be reduced to a minor power, and thus reduced we will not survive—nor will freedom or Western values survive.

The United States certainly wished to have it both ways: to retain some semblance of the world structure that it inherited from the nineteenth century (enough, that is to say, to support strong alliances between former colonial powers, the majority of which continued to identify themselves as allies within the "free world"), and at the same time, to make certain that the contest with the Soviet Union would be played out in its favor.

As it happened, the beginning of strong United States involvement in Vietnam coincides exactly with the beginning of the construction of this postwar U.S. foreign policy. Similarly, the period in which the United States' presence was felt in Vietnam—from September 2, 1945, to May 1, 1975—coincides exactly with the period in which these foreign-policy objectives were being enunciated. Thus it was to be expected that American policy toward Vietnam would reflect the tension between these two competing principles....

Altruism *and* Competition

Ostensibly, America had not become active in Vietnam to promote selfish ambitions, to advance its own desires, or even to protect its vested interests. All that it attempted could be justified on the basis of the cardinal principle—the need to maintain a stable and benevolent world order.

Unfortunately, this professed altruistic motive became hopelessly entangled with the discordant twin objective of winning the competition with the rival power center. Before long, it became inevitable that the second objective would be taken as the means to insure the realization of the first. An expectation grew that stable world order could be achieved if the United States could win the contest with the Soviet Union, now simply referred to as the adversary. Logically speaking, the two principles were interdependent from the very moment following the end of the Second World War when foreign policy was being reformulated....

Leader of the World

Inexorably, the decisions [about Vietnam] reflected America's idea of its global role—a view that the United States could not recoil from world leadership.

Stanley Karnow, *Vietnam: A History*, 1983.

Accordingly, when crucial choices were placed before American decision-makers, the outcome was inevitable. Certainly most U.S. Presidents wished to have it both ways—to keep the two objectives in harmony and balance. When they couldn't, however—when the twin ambitions became manifestly incompatible and contradictory—the leaders found most support in advancing the American cause against its primary competition. No American President could afford politically to be soft on communism, so each felt obliged to push the get-tough policy to prominence. In doing so, each allowed the ideological struggle to assume critical and strategic dominance, and whenever this occurred, the "patriotic temper" (promoting "the politics of national assertion") gained mastery over the "inward-looking politics of compassionate reform.'' The same temper won out in the leaders' attitude toward the nation's involvement in Vietnam: Vietnam was the testing ground not simply for the free-enterprise system, but for the conflict in American will and resolve, manifested for the entire world, including the American citizenry.

Polarization

If the United States had not invested the situation in Vietnam with rivalry with Communist powers, the tragedy might have been avoided. If it had perceived the conflict as a civil war, it would have had no good reason to become involved. If it had seen the situation simply as a clash between colonialists and nationalists, it might not have entered military engagement. But because it viewed the war as part of the fundamental conflict between the world's two great superpowers, the United States eventually felt a responsibility to commit its forces. The quality and intensity of that commitment was nurtured by the religious sanctions of the patriotic temper and the Manichaean mythology by which the rivalry was expressed. In this rendition, America was placed on the side of good, in opposition to evil. Light was pitted against darkness, freedom against bondage, America against anti-America—yes, even God against the Devil.

Within a relatively brief span of time, therefore, the postwar world became sharply polarized, exhibiting all of the characteristic invitations for takeover by an Armageddon mentality. By the time of the Gulf of Tonkin Resolution in 1964, the way had been cleared by Korea in 1950, the Berlin blockade in 1961, and the Cuban missile crisis in 1963. All of these challenges had been met successfully, to America's advantage. Vietnam was simply next in the series. The nation could be confident that the problem would be solved in a relatively short time. But by now the equations were inexact.

To be sure, Ho Chi Minh espoused the Communist philosophy and had strong loyalties to both China and the Soviet Union. He had been trained in the teachings of Marx and Lenin and was thoroughly committed to Marxist thought and the Communist social and political program. Yet the plot the Americans envisioned bore only generalized application to the actual drama in Vietnam. U.S. leadership tried to direct the scenes with little or no knowledge of local circumstances and incentives. It tried to erect in South Vietnam a government which the people clearly resisted. It wished to promote certain Western forms of democratic decision-making among a people who had had no preparation and had shown no strong inclinations for them. It possessed only slight acquaintance with the indigenous sociocultural matrix, based on a combination of Confucian, Taoist, Buddhist, and native religious influences and organized according to ancient Chinese mandarinic systems. It was as if the plot had been written by someone who had not yet visited the territory and had been imposed much more because of the plight of the outsiders than because it concerned the affairs of the Vietnamese.

Misguided Goals

Stanley Hoffmann, a Harvard specialist in international government, describes American military and political hubris in Vietnam this way:

> The central problem of American policy—of any policy—is the relevance of its ends to specific cases: the more ambitious or ideological a policy, the more indispensable it is to analyze the realities of each case with critical rigor before applying to it one's concepts or preconceptions, for otherwise the statesmen will trip into the pitfalls of irrelevance, "adventurism," or unreality.

Fear of Losing Face

Thus the primary consideration soon became not the importance of a noncommunist South Vietnam in itself but the repercussions to be expected from reneging on this commitment. As concerns the impact internationally, the fear was of disillusionment with the worth of the alliances contracted by the U.S. and the encouragement of other Communist-led "wars of national liberation" which might follow a retreat from Southeast Asia. With regard to the domestic scene, the steadfast defense of South Vietnam was to preempt the charge of being soft on communism, an accusation to which Democratic presidents, mindful of Yalta and the "loss of China," were particularly senstive.

Guenter Lewy, *America in Vietnam*, 1978.

He continues:

> Our own policy was of necessity ambitious because of our very role as a superpower; and it has, if not an ideology, at least a set of principles and dogmas such as resistance to aggression, attachment to self-determination, opposition to forceful communist takeovers, etc....
>
> *The tragedy of our course in Vietnam lies in our refusal to come to grips with those realities in South Vietnam that happened to be decisive from the viewpoint of politics.*

Understandably, all such ventures are doomed to failure because they embody the expectation that the structure and order of the world can be established and maintained if the United States achieves success in its contest with its chief rival.

Beguiled and misshaped by the full weight of the mythological anticipation—that it was a righteous cause and that righteousness should prevail—the military venture was confutable from the first.

"The decision makers made one crucial mistake:. . .They 'underestimated the resistance and the determination of the North Vietnamese.'"

Underestimating the Enemy Caused Defeat

John Mueller

John Mueller is a professor of political science at the University of Rochester in New York. He received a Ph.D. from UCLA. He specializes in the areas of international politics, foreign policy, and defense policy. Mr. Mueller has conducted extensive research on the Viet Nam war and has published numerous papers on that subject. In the following viewpoint, he contends that the US involvement in Vietnam was well thought out but the determination and fanaticism of the enemy was underestimated.

As you read, consider the following questions:

1. Why, according to the author, was there a special urgency to Vietnam's position in 1965 that contributed to the United States' unfortunate intervention there?
2. What does Mr. Mueller mean by "the extraordinary fanaticism of the enemy"?

John Mueller, "Vietnam Involvement Was a Failure, Not a Folly," *Wall Street Journal*, April 10, 1984. Reprinted by permission of *Wall Street Journal*, © Dow Jones & Company, Inc., 1984. All rights reserved.

In her new best-selling book, *The March of Folly*, Barbara W. Tuchman assesses several historical instances in which, as she sees it, "folly" was committed: Decision makers acted contrary "to the way reason points and enlightened self-interest suggests." Her most extensively discussed example is the American decision to "betray herself in Vietnam." Successive administrations should have known their policy was doomed to failure, she argues, and had the "moral courage" to reverse course.

With the blessings of hindsight—something Mrs. Tuchman sternly eschews early in her book—we now know that U.S. policy in Vietnam was a tragic mistake. But a decision should not be judged for reasonableness simply according to its success or failure, but according to the process by which it was made. All important decisions contain an irreducible amount of uncertainty and guesswork, and nobody succeeds all the time. What we can sensibly demand of decision makers, whether they be presidents or stock market analysts, is that they carefully assess their values, examine alternatives and pursue the strategy with the best probability of success.

Carefully Considered Action

By these standards, the American intervention into the war in Vietnam was far from a case of folly; it may well have been one of the most fully considered, carefully reasoned actions in our history. And thus the gloomy lesson is that failure could have been prevented only by dumb luck, not by more enlightened decision making.

Pivotal, of course, was the decision in 1965 to send vast numbers of American troops to take over the war effort and to prevent what seemed to be an imminent collapse of the South Vietnamese military. This decision process went on for months, and extensive documentation on it is available. The evidence suggests that the leaders did all the right things: They evaluated fundamental values and premises, they assessed possible alternatives and they came up with a strategy with reasonable promise of success.

In 1965 there was a broad consensus, both within the government and without, that Vietnam was, in reporter David Halberstam's assessment at the time, "a strategic country in a key area...—one of only five or six nations in the world that is truly vital to U.S. interests." As Mrs. Tuchman observes, this was an extension of the policy of containing international communism that had guided American policy in the postwar era (and still does, for the most part). What she fails to appreciate is that there was a special urgency to Vietnam's position in 1965: Communist China to the north was crowing belligerently about aiding and encouraging other Vietnams around the globe, while the huge island republic of Indonesia to the south was gradually locking itself into a semi-alliance with China. (Within a year or two, after masses of American troops were committed to Vietnam, these conditions were to change radically: There was a violent anti-Communist coup in Indonesia; and China, its foreign policy an almost universal failure, was to turn northward to dispute with the Soviet Union, as well as inward to embark on that bizarre, self-destructive ritual of purification known as the Cultural Revolution. But U.S. decision makers could hardly have known in 1965 that this was going to happen.)

What is impressive about the decision making of 1965 is not that the containment consensus prevailed, but that those holding this view were so willing to entertain fundamental challenges to their position. In a tightly reasoned argument Undersecretary of State George Ball attacked the application of the containment policy to Vietnam and urged judicious withdrawal. Moreover, Mr. Ball's position, which was far more radical than almost anything heard at the time outside the government, was not stifled at low levels but allowed to percolate to the top; as Mrs. Tuchman observes, Mr. Ball went through the argument point by point with the man ultimately responsible, President Lyndon Johnson.

Mysterious Enemy

I am more convinced than before that the United States could never have won a conflict in this alien land, where the enemy was tenacious, dedicated—and everywhere. . . .

In short, the Vietnam conflict was waged in an environment too complex and mysterious for Americans to comprehend.

Stanley Karnow, *Minneapolis Tribune*, May 11, 1981.

Mr. Ball's argument was rejected not out of whim or myopia, but because the others decided, after careful reflection, that Vietnam really was a vital interest and that, though risky, the infusion of American troops was the best policy. As part of this consideration, thoughtful assessments were made of the probable U.S. casualty rates over the next couple of years—estimates that proved to be quite accurate. It is doubtful that American decision making upon entering World War II showed such careful, fully rounded consideration of essential values and probable costs.

"Wooden-Headedness"?

In all this, the decision makers made one crucial mistake: As Secretary of State Dean Rusk observed in 1971, they "underestimated the resistance and the determination of the North Vietnamese." Mrs. Tuchman ascribes this mistake to "wooden-headedness," but the lessons of the past suggest the misestimation was highly reasonable: The willingness of the Communists to accept punishment in Vietnam was virtually unprecedented in the history of modern warfare.

If one takes the hundreds of participating countries in international and colonial wars since 1816 and calculates for each the battle death rate as a percentage of the pre-war population, it quickly becomes apparent that Vietnam was an extreme case. Even discounting heavily for exaggerations in the "body count," the Communist side was willing to accept battle death rates that were twice as high as those accepted by the fanatical, often suicidal Japanese in World War II. Indeed, the few combatants who took losses as high as the Vietnamese Communists were mainly those such as the Germans and Soviets in World War II who were fighting to the death—for their national existence—not merely for expansion like North Vietnam.

The failure of American decision makers to appreciate the extraordinary fanaticism of the enemy is hardly evidence of "woodenheadedness." Mrs. Tuchman suggests the U.S. should have taken the warnings of various French leaders on this issue. But French military history in the last century or so, fraught with inept leadership, precipitous collapse and mutiny, hardly made the advice seem very credible. Anyway, even the French had been able to control the area for decades against local resistance, and in 1954 they had been able to get the Communists in Indochina to accept a peaceful partition, a reasonable halfloaf, after inflicting casualties vastly lower than those delivered by the Americans a decade later. Moreover there were many relevant instances of successful wars against Communist insurgencies: In Malaya in 1960, in the Philippines in 1954, in Greece in 1949, dedicated Communist forces gave up or faded away after being substantially battered; why would one necessarily expect the Vietnamese Communists to be different?

Thus the war can be condemned as a mistake, but not a "folly." Decision makers knew what they were doing, often reassessed their premises, compared possible policy alternatives and tried their best to predict the outcome. If there was "folly," it was in Hanoi, where the leadership (made "paranoid" by U.S. bombing, explains Mrs. Tuchman) relentlessly sent its youth to the south to be ground up by the American war machine without, it appears, a serious evaluation of the relationship between potential gain and inevitable cost, or of alternative, less costly strategies.

"At the center...was a failure to decide clearly whether the problem was primarily an internal insurgency or an aggression."

Poorly Planned Strategy Caused Defeat

Norman Hannah

Norman Hannah, a retired foreign service officer, served in various capacities connected to Southeast Asia from 1947 to 1970. In the following viewpoint he states that US leaders were unable to decide the nature of the war. This led to confused and ineffective strategies.

As you read, consider the following questions:

1. What does Mr. Hannah mean when he talks about a "fatal schizoid deception that distorted our intelligence estimates"?
2. Why did neutralization fail?
3. Why was time a crucial factor in US failure in Vietnam?

Norman Hannah, "Vietnam Deception—Not Conspiracy, But Indecision," *The Washington Times*, September 30, 1982. © *The Washington Times*, 1982. Reprinted with permission.

Which is more important? How the U.S. failed in Vietnam? Or whether CBS unfairly charged "conspiracy" in the reporting of intelligence data on enemy strength in Vietnam? Clearly, the latter, to judge from the fascinating dust-up summarized by Glenn Garvin in *The Washington Times.*

This is too bad because whatever errors and abuses it committed, CBS' controversial documentary uncovered a fatal schizoid deception that distorted our intelligence estimates. In so doing, CBS caught one end of a long thread which flawed our whole enterprise in Indochina, a thread which, if pursued, leads all the way back to 1961 when the principal lines of our strategy were laid down.

With its hasty, attention-getting charge of conspiracy, CBS dropped the thread of the real story of why the war was lost. Perhaps it is too much to hope that the current flap might stimulate a serendipitous return to the main theme, but it is unfair to leave the U.S. Military—Gen. Westmoreland, in particular—twisting alone in a web woven by people and forces beyond their control as much as 20 years ago.

Failure to Decide

At the center of the web was a failure to decide clearly whether the problem was primarily an internal insurgency or an aggression. President Kennedy himself talked sometimes of aggression and sometimes of civil war. Which did he believe? Roger Hilsman, former assistant secretary of state for the Far East under Kennedy, writes that, "The president preferred to treat the problem of Vietnam as something other than war." But what? Hilsman doesn't say. But this reflects a dangerous ambivalence. Splitting the difference between opposites is often possible in politics but when the stage of possible war has been reached the gray shading must give way to definite choice. Unfortunately, the by-word of the day was, "Keep your options open."

The ambivalence of the president spread throughout the government. As late as 1965, when we were already committing U.S. ground forces, President Johnson and Secretaries Rusk and McNamara were publicly wrestling with the dilemma. The chairman of the Joint Chiefs of Staff, Gen. Wheeler, thought, "the essence of the problem is military." Averell Harriman, Hilsman and White House aide Forrestal saw the problem, in Hilsman's words, "as one of civil war rather than external aggression." Walt Rostow saw a major threat in Hanoi's infiltration through Laos. But, according to Hilsman, Kennedy regarded the infiltration trails through Laos as a political trap, "a built-in excuse for failure" (rather than a built-in cause of failure.)

Gen. Maxwell Taylor supported counter-insurgency doctrine and recommended more advisers and helicopters but, ambivalently, along with these he recommended deployment of some 8,000 U.S. troops in the autumn of 1961. Equally ambivalently, President Kennedy approved the advisers and helicopters but, in a familiar Washington political gambit, reserved judgement on the troops while allowing the planning for deployment to go ahead.

Vulnerable President

The confusion started in the aftermath of the Bay of Pigs when President Kennedy adopted separate strategies toward Laos and Vietnam. After the Cuban disaster he felt too vulnerable at home to undertake commitments in distant, landlocked Laos where North Vietnamese forces, with Soviet support, were taking advantage of a boiling internal struggle.

Military Confusion

It was the job of military professionals to judge the true nature of the Vietnam War, to communicate the facts to our civilian decision makers, and to recommend appropriate strategies. . . . It is indicative of our strategic failure in Vietnam that so many years after our involvement the true nature of the Vietnam War is still in question. . . .

To have understood the true nature of the Vietnam War not only required a strict definition of the enemy, it also required a knowledge of the nature of war itself. Our understanding was clouded by confusion over preparation for war and the conduct of war, by fears of nuclear war, by fears of Chinese intervention, and by the misconception that we were being challenged by a whole new kind of "revolutionary" war that could be countered only by the "strategy" of counterinsurgency.

Harry G. Summers Jr., *Society*, November/December 1983.

But at the same time he felt too vulnerable to appear supine and hence needed to act vigorously in South Vietnam which offered greater possibilities and seemingly less risk. To accomplish this straddle, he decided to accept Averell Harriman's judgement and negotiate with the USSR toward the neutralization of Laos while embarking on a vigorous internal support campaign in South Vietnam in accordance with the new "counter-insurgency" doctrine then being hammered out.

Neutralization was the link between the different strategies in Laos and South Vietnam. If neutralization worked, that would cut Hanoi's logistical link to South Vietnam which could then be handled as an internal problem. And the administration need not risk the backlash of the Bay of Pigs.

As a short term tactic to gain time this had merit but we had no longer range strategy and we became frozen in the rigid pattern of the hollow facade of neutralization. The agreements on Laos failed the day they were signed because Laos became Hanoi's invasion route to South Vietnam. We became frozen in a strategy which:

1. Prevented using US forces to stop the aggression through Laos;

2. Required pouring more and more men and arms into South Vietnam to pacify its countryside against invaders who continued to stream in through Laos.

So we were involved in an internal pacification where we shouldn't have been and we were not deployed to stop the aggression where it occurred which is the only place we should have been in military force. Small wonder there was confusion and disagreement over what we were doing and whom we were fighting.

No Front Line

We never developed a front line in Vietnam because we never decided to confront the enemy in his primary role as aggressor (in Laos) but waited until he had assumed his spurious "insurgent" role in South Vietnam. A front line concentrated both sides in a narrow area which simplified the obtaining and interpreting of intelligence. The Vietnam war was a war of statistics. Lacking a front line to measure progress or loss, our only measure was by the continuous digestion and regurgitation of statistics.

In this way, the amorphous nature of our strategy contributed to the quarrel over intelligence estimates which, after all, was the subject of the CBS report. It is not necessary to postulate a conspiracy. In fact, to do so detracts from the real question which is—did we know and agree on what we were trying to do *and how* we were trying to do it? The answer is clearly, "No!" Naturally, different sides will report and emphasize those statistics which prove their respective points of view. And they did.

Was it more important to suppress the enemy already in South Vietnam or to close the route by which reinforcements were coming? If one emphasizes the internal war already in existence, then the enemy within must be suppressed first, such as the village para-military which Adams and Allen of CIA wanted to include and Gen. Westmoreland wanted to exclude.

But, if one emphasizes the external aggression, then it was more important to close the external reinforcement route by which up to 20,000 or 25,000 North Vietnamese forces were arriving every one of the autumn months of 1967 leading up to the Tet Offensive of January 1968.

Too Long a Wait

But there is a critical linkage between the two propositions. The longer we wait to deal with the external route of reinforcement, the more severe becomes the internal problem, thereby making it even more difficult to get away from the pressing internal threat. And this is what happened to us—we waited and waited and then it was too late.

Gen. Westmoreland said, in his press conference after the CBS report, that he had told President Johnson in March 1967 that, "the war could go on indefinitely if the U.S. did not cut the infiltration trails through Laos." In his book *A Soldier Reports,* he says he had prepared plans for cutting the trails, a project which he says both Ambassadors Lodge and Bunker favored. But, he went on to say, the operation would require three divisions and, "I would be unable for a long time to spare that many troops from the critical fight *within* South Vietnam."

Unclear Objectives

In his analysis of the Vietnam War (*The War Managers*, University Press of New England), Brigadier General Douglas Kinnard found that "almost seventy percent of the Army generals who managed the war were uncertain of its objectives." . . .

Former Secretary of Defense Clark Clifford testified that when he took over in 1968, no one could tell him what constituted "victory," no one could tell him our plan to end the war. This was a fatal deficiency, for as Clausewitz had warned,

No one starts a war—or rather, no one in his senses ought to do so—without first being clear in his mind what he intends to achieve by that war and how he intends to conduct it.

Harry G. Summers Jr., *The New Republic*, July 12, 1982.

In effect, he was giving the internal suppression priority over closure of the external route of aggression without taking account of the fact that by so doing he was allowing time to work against him. He confirmed this later when he told us that after the Tet Offensive the enemy was depleted but, unfortunately, by then time had run out on the president back in Washington and he could not act.

I recall a Honolulu conference in 1966 at Pacific Command headquarters, when the subject was how to increase our rate of attrition of infiltration. Afterward, I asked Gen. Westmoreland what he would do if the enemy would simply increase his *input* of infiltration at the top end of the Laos trails enough to offset the attrition that we inflicted so that the *output* in South Vietnam did not fall or even increased.

"We'll just continue to grind them up as we are doing," he replied, grimly. The figure of speech was apt. Our strategy was often described as a "meatgrinder." The question was: Who would tire first, he who feeds the machine or he who grinds? The test was settled at the Tet Offensive. We, the grinders, tired first.

Far more than the media's pursuit of its own in-house narcissistic-masochistic fight over its own ethics, it is important to pick up the thread of contradictory intelligence estimates and roll it back to its origin in a failure at the top in Washington to decide. By opening this Pandora's box we might recover our self-confidence and hope.

"For the first time in modern history, the outcome of a war was determined not on the battlefield but on the printed page."

US Journalists Caused Defeat

Robert Elegant

Robert Elegant was a foreign correspondent and commentator and, in his words, "a participant as well as an observer in the Viet Nam imbroglio from 1955 to 1975." He covered the war for *Newsweek* and the *Los Angeles Times/Washington Post* News Service. Until 1965 he opposed US military intervention in Vietnam. He then changed his mind because of the need he saw to contain a potentially aggressive Chinese expansionist foreign policy. In the following viewpoint he presents his reasons for claiming that the defeat of South Vietnam can be largely blamed on his fellow journalists.

As you read, consider the following questions:

1. In Mr. Elegant's opinion, for whom did reporters covering the Vietnam war write?
2. What role does the author say television played in Vietnam?
3. Why, according to Mr. Elegant, did Western journalists deceive themselves about the nature of the "liberation of Indochina"?

Robert Elegant, "How to Lose a War: Reflections of a Foreign Correspondent," *Encounter*, August 1981. Reprinted with permission.

In the early 1960s, when the Viet Nam War became a big story, most foreign correspondents assigned to cover the story wrote primarily to win the approbation of the crowd, above all their own crowd. As a result, in my view, the self-proving system of reporting they created became ever further detached from political and military realities because it instinctively concentrated on its own self-justification. The American press, naturally dominant in an "American war," somehow felt obliged to be less objective than partisan, to take sides, for it was inspired by the *engagé* "investigative" reporting that burgeoned in the United States in these impassioned years. The press was instinctively "agin the government"—and, at least reflexively, for Saigon's enemies.

During the latter half of the fifteen-year American involvement in Viet Nam, the media became the primary battlefield. Illusory events reported *by* the press as well as real events *within* the press corps were more decisive than the clash of arms or the contention of ideologies. For the first time in modern history, the outcome of a war was determined not on the battlefield but on the printed page and, above all, on the television screen. Looking back coolly, I believe it can be said (surprising as it may still sound) that South Vietnamese and American forces actually won the limited military struggle. They virtually crushed the Viet Cong in the South, the "native" guerrillas who were directed, reinforced, and equipped from Hanoi; and thereafter they threw back the invasion by regular North Vietnamese divisions. Nonetheless, the war was finally lost to the invaders *after* the U.S. disengagement because the political pressures built up by the media had made it quite impossible for Washington to maintain even the minimal material and moral support that would have enabled the Saigon regime to continue effective resistance....

The Brotherhood

In my own personal experience most correspondents *wanted* to talk chiefly to other correspondents to confirm their own *mythical* vision of the war. Even newcomers were precommitted, as the American jargon has it, to the collective position most of their colleagues had already taken. What I can only call surrealistic reporting constantly fed on itself, and did not diminish thereby, but swelled into ever more grotesque shapes. I found the process equally reprehensible for being in no small part unwitting....

Most correspondents were isolated from the Vietnamese by ignorance of their language and culture, as well as by a measure of race estrangement. Most were isolated from the quixotic American Army establishment, itself often as confused as they themselves were, by their moralistic attitudes and their political prejudices. It was inevitable, in the circumstances, that they came to write, in the first instance, for each other....

After each other, correspondents wrote to win the approbation of their editors, who controlled their professional lives and who were closely linked with the intellectual community at home. The consensus of that third circle, the domestic intelligentsia, derived largely from correspondents' reports and in turn served to determine the nature of those reports. If dispatches did not accord with that consensus, approbation was withheld. Only in the last instance did correspondents address themselves to the general public, the mass of lay readers and viewers....

Maximum Reportage

Because there was no declared war, maximum freedom of reportage was permitted from the battlefield. (At one point, there were some 500 American newsmen and TV operators in Vietnam, each striving for the type of sensational story that would yield a by-line or several minutes on the tube.) War as suppertime entertainment entered its mature phase....

Not only did reporters generally lack experience and an in-depth understanding of the complexities of Asian politics, they also did what came naturally—sought the most sensational angle. And there was no small amount of political bias, fortified by their being able to see all the corruption, inefficiency, and divisions of the "ins," but not being able to assess the shortcomings of the "outs."

Robert A. Scalapino, *Society*, November/December 1983.

Not surprisingly, one found that most reporting veered farther and farther from the fundamental political, economic, and military realities of the war, for these were usually *not* spectacular. Reporting Viet Nam became a closed, self-generating system sustained largely by the acclaim the participants lavished on each other in almost equal measure to the opprobrium they heaped on "the Establishment," a fashionable and very vulnerable target.

The Cloud of Unknowing

For some journalists, perhaps most, a moment of truth through self-examination was never to come. The farther they were from the real conflict, the more smugly self-approving they now remain as commentators who led the public to expect a brave new world when the North Vietnamese finally "liberated" South Viet Nam. Even those correspondents who today gingerly confess to some errors or distortions usually insist that the true fault was not theirs at all, but Washington's. The enormity of having helped in one way or another to bring tens of millions under grinding totalitarian rule—and having tilted the global balance of power—appears too great to acknowledge. It is easier to absolve one's self by blaming exclusively Johnson, Nixon, and Kissinger.

I found few American correspondents to be as tough-minded as one Briton I knew who was very close to the action for many years in the employ of an American wire-news service. "I'm ashamed of most of what I wrote in Viet Nam," he told me recently. "But I was a new boy, and I took my lead from the Americans, who were afire with the crusading spirit of '60s journalism—the involvement, man, in the good fight. When I look at what's happened now, I'm ashamed of my ignorance—and what I helped to do to the Vietnamese....

Journalistic institutions are, of course, rarely afflicted by false modesty. They have not disclaimed credit for the outcome of the war, and their representatives have taken public bows for their successful intervention. The multitude of professional prizes bestowed upon the "bi-story" coverage of Viet Nam certainly implied approval of the general effort.

Media's Key Role

However, the media have been rather coy; they have not declared that they played a *key* role in the conflict. They have not proudly trumpeted Hanoi's repeated expressions of gratitude to the mass media of the non-Communist world, although Hanoi has indeed affirmed that it could not have won "without the Western press." The Western press appears either unaware of the direct connection between cause (its reporting) and effect (the Western defeat in Viet Nam), or strangely reluctant to proclaim that the pen and the camera proved decisively mightier than the bayonet and ultra-modern weapons.

Nor have the media dwelt upon the glaring inconsistency between the expectation they raised of peaceful, prosperous development after Saigon's collapse and the present post-war circumstances in Indochina....

Any searching analysis of fundamental premises has remained as unthinkable to "the critics" as it was during the fighting. They have remained committed to the proposition that the American role in Indochina was totally reprehensible and inexcusable, while the North Vietnamese role—and, by extension, the roles of the Khmer Rouge in Cambodia and the Pathet Lao in Laos—was righteous, magnanimous, and just. Even the growing number who finally deplored the repressive consequences of the totalitarian victory could not bring themselves to re-examine the premises that led them to contribute so decisively to those victories. Thus William Shawcross, before his sententious book, *Sideshow,* wrote of the Communists' reshaping of Cambodian society: "The process is atrociously brutal." Although "the Khmer people are suffering horribly under their new rules," this is how Shawcross unhesitatingly assigned the ultimate blame:

84

Don Wright, *Miami News*. Reprinted with permission.

> They have suffered every day of the last six years—ever since the begin-
> ning of one of the most destructive foreign policies the United States has
> ever pursued: the "Nixon-Kissinger doctrine" in its purest form....

Most correspondents on the scene were not quite as vehement.
But they were moved by the same conviction of American guilt,
which was so fixed that it resisted all the evidence pointing to a
much more complex reality. Employed in the service of that
crusading fervor was, for the first time, the most emotionally
moving medium of all.

Television, its thrusting and simplistic character shaping its
message, was most shocking because it was most immediate.
The Viet Nam War was a presence in homes throughout the
world. Who could seriously doubt the veracity of so plausible
and so moving a witness in one's own living room?

At any given moment, a million images were available to the
camera's lens in Saigon alone—and hundreds of millions
throughout Indochina. But TV crews naturally perferred the
most dramatic. That, after all, was their business—show
business. It was not news to film farmers peacefully tilling their
rice fields, though it might have been argued that nothing happening *was* news when the American public had been led to
believe that almost every Vietnamese farmer was regularly
threatened by the Viet Cong, constantly imperiled by battle, and
rarely safe from indiscriminate U.S. bombing.

A few hard, documented instances. A burning village was
news, even though it was a deserted village used in a Marine
training exercise—even though the television correspondent had
handed his Zippo lighter to a non-commissioned officer with the

suggestion that he set fire to an abandoned house. American soldiers cutting ears off a Viet Cong corpse was news—even if the cameraman, had offered the soldiers his knife and "dared" them to take those grisly souvenirs....

The Reasons Why

The main question persists. Why was the press—whether in favor of official policy at the beginning or vehemently against the war at the end—so superficial and so biased?

Chief among many reasons was, I believe, the politicization of correspondents by the constantly intensifying clamor over Viet Nam in Europe and America. Amateur (and professional) propagandists served both sides of the question, but the champions of Hanoi were spectacularly more effective. They created an atmosphere of high pressure that made it exceedingly difficult to be objective....

A Naive Expectation

Many newcomers were shocked to find that American and Vietnamese briefing officers did not always tell them the truth even about a minor tactical situation. Despite their pose of professional skepticism, in their naivete they expected those officers to tell not merely the truth but the *whole* truth. Far from feeling the deep mistrust of officialdom they affected, the newcomers were dismayed by the briefing officers' inability (or unwillingness) to confide in them unreservedly. Older correspondents did not expect candor from briefing officers. They had learned several wars earlier that the interests of the press and the interests of the military did not normally coincide. They also knew that the briefing officers were themselves often uninformed—concerned, perhaps sometimes excessively, for military secrecy—and resentful of correspondents' badgering....

Official deceit was thus exacerbated by incompetent journalism. While complaining about the press, many U.S. officials, who knew they were fighting "a media war," sought to manipulate—rather than inform—correspondents. But they were not skilled at manipulation. While complaining about the government's duplicity, many editors assigned correspondents who were not qualified to fill a normal foreign post, much less to thread the labyrinthine complexities of the Indochina War. Some editors told their correspondents what they wanted, while many correspondents had made up their own minds before they arrived "in country."...

Beyond the pressures exerted upon them, most correspondents—serving six-month to two-year tours—were woefully ignorant of the setting of the conflict. Some strove diligently to remedy that crippling deficiency by reading widely and interviewing avidly. Many lacked the time or the inclination to do so—or any real awareness of how crippling their ignorance was to them professionally....

Despite their own numerous and grave faults, the South Vietnamese were, first and last, decisively defeated in Washington, New York, London, and Paris. Those media defeats made inevitable their subsequent defeat on the battlefield. Indochina was not perhaps the first major conflict to be won by psychological warfare. But it was probably the first to be lost by psychological warfare conducted at such great physical distance from the actual fields of battle—and so far from the peoples whose fate was determined by the outcome of the conflict.

Locating Scapegoats

During World War Two the Nazis in Germany systematically killed millions of Jews. The Nazis continually propagandized the outrageous lie that Jews were responsible for many of Germany's social problems. Jews became the victims of irrational leaders who glorified force, violence, and the doctrines of racial supremacy. One of the principal propaganda weapons used against the Jews by Germany's leaders was the tactic of scapegoating.

On an individual level scapegoating involves the process of transferring personal blame or anger to another individual or object. Most people, for example, have kicked their table or chair as an outlet for anger and frustration over a mistake or failure. *On a group level, scapegoating involves the placement of blame on entire groups of people or objects for social problems that they have not caused.* Scapegoats may be totally or only partially innocent, but they always receive more blame than can be rationally justified.

The cartoon on the next page illustrates a vicious example of scapegoating, using blacks as the victims. Unfortunately scapegoating is still a common practice.

"IF YOU PEOPLE HAD MORE ABORTIONS, OUR POLICE WOULD HAVE AN EASIER JOB."

Muhammed Speaks, April 20, 1975.

Because societies are so complex and complicated, problems are often not completely understood by any single citizen. Yet people always demand answers and there exists a human tendency to create imaginary and simplistic explanations for complex racial, social, economic, and political problems that defy easy understanding and solution. The Vietnam War falls into this category. During the war Americans could not agree on the reasons for involvement. Since the war's end, Americans cannot agree on the reasons for its dismal conclusion. Both situations provide fertile ground for scapegoating.

Part 1

Step 1.   The class should break into groups of four to six students. Each small group should examine the cartoon carefully and discuss why it is an example of scapegoating.

89

Step 2.   The small groups should next examine the following
            statements. Each group should mark the statements
            in the following fashion. *Mark S for any statement that
            the group decides is an example of scapegoating. Mark NS
            for any statement that is not an example of scapegoating.
            Mark U for statements for which determination is undecid-
            ed or unsure.*

            S = *an example of scapegoating*
            NS = *not an example of scapegoating*
            U = *undecided or unsure*

1. Communists are responsible for most of the world's war and
   violence.

2. Biased journalists bear major responsibility for America's
   failure in Vietnam.

3. Capitalism is more dependent on the profit motive than is
   communism.

4. President Johnson was responsible for sending the most US
   combat troops to Vietnam.

5. Antiwar demonstrators pressured American leaders to
   withdraw US troops from Vietnam.

6. Undisciplined black soldiers were responsible for America's
   loss in Vietnam.

7. Corrupt Saigon allies were responsible for the fall of South
   Vietnam.

8. Liberals in American society and government undermined
   US efforts in Vietnam and are responsible for the
   communist victory.

Step 3.   Each small group should compare its results with other
            groups in a classwide discussion.

Periodical Bibliography

The following list of periodical articles deals with the subject matter of this chapter.

M. Stanton Evans   "Why US Suffered Defeat in Vietnam," *Human Events*, September 30, 1975.

James Fallows   "M-16: A Bureaucratic Horror Story," *The Atlantic Monthly*, June 1981.

Norman Hannah   "Now We Know," *National Review*, June 11, 1976.

H.J. Kaplan   "With the American Press in Vietnam," *Commentary*, May 1982.

Eugene W. Massengale   "We Did Not Lose in Vietnam," *Worldview*, December 1975.

Norman Podhoretz   "Vietnam: The Revised Standard Version," *Commentary*, April 1984.

Society   Special section on "Vietnam as Unending Trauma," November/December 1983.

What Are the Consequences of Vietnam?

> *"Those on both sides of the Vietnam conflict were exposed to and participated in consciousness-altering, irreversible, massive evil."*

The War Defiled the American Conscience

William P. Mahedy

William P. Mahedy is Episcopal campus minister at the University of California-San Diego in La Jolla and at San Diego State University. In the following viewpoint Mr. Mahedy writes that US involvement in Vietnam destroyed the national sense of innocence and, thus, the nation's faith in itself.

As you read, consider the following questions:

1. What American myths does the author say were destroyed by the Vietnam war?
2. How does he say the destruction of these myths has affected the nation?

William P. Mahedy, "'It Don't Mean Nothin': The Vietnam Experience." Copyright 1984 Christian Century Foundation. Reprinted by permission from the January 26, 1983 issue of *The Christian Century*.

"When I went to Vietnam, I believed in Jesus Christ and John Wayne. After Vietnam, both went down the tubes. It don't mean nothin'." Though I have heard other veterans say the same thing a thousand times in different ways, this statement made by a vet in a rap group is, for me, the most concise unmasking of American civil religion and its mythology of war. The loss of faith and meaning experienced by countless Vietnam veterans is now widely known, despite the best efforts of the religious and political right to incorporate Vietnam into the classical mythology of war. If the United States government is to rearm the country for the struggle against "godless communism"—including preparation for a protracted nuclear war—it must first encourage the remythologizing of America. Foreign policy must be consistent with our national myth: we are God's chosen people in all that we undertake. We believe America has a divine mandate to evangelize the world to its own political and economic systems. War is the sacred instrument, the great cultic activity, whereby this mission is achieved. Jesus Christ and John Wayne must again be linked after their brief separation by Vietnam.

We Cannot Admit the Truth

President Reagan has declared the Vietnam war a noble cause and the right wing has unleashed its fury against those who question the traditional mythology. The Reagan administration's attempt to dismantle the controversial Vietnam Veterans' Outreach Program shortly after taking office was consistent with this remythologizing: If the administration were to admit that the last war caused serious psychological, moral and spiritual problems, then it would be more difficult to prepare the public for a similar conflict or for a much larger conflagration. The truth about the pain, anger and disillusionment of the Vietnam veterans cannot be admitted if one espouses the traditional American civil religion. Having invested our political and cultural systems with religious characteristics, we must necessarily interpret our historical experience in terms of a sacred dimension. We must forever remain the chosen people, the "city on the hill" of our myth of origin. We cannot wage mere wars; we must fight crusades against the infidels....

The Vietnam war provided no transcendent meaning by which the national purpose could be reinterpreted and transposed into a new key. War was, for the first time in American history, experienced by great numbers of its participants as sin. Psychotherapy is uneasy with the notion of sin, as are most Americans of the late 20th century. As a result, much of what the veterans have to say cannot even be articulated, much less understood. The language and the concepts they need no longer exist within the arena of public discourse.

94

REBUILDING VIETNAM

Roy Justus in *The Minneapolis Star*.

A large segment of the American religious community (which does possess the linguistic and philosophical tools necessary to deal with the moral and religious questions raised by Vietnam) chooses not to see the war as sin. In *The Unfinished War: Vietnam and the American Conscience* (Beacon, 1982), Walter Capps argues that the "rise of Protestant conservatism...or the new religious right bears direct connection with individual and corporate wrestling over the ramifications of the Vietnam experience." Viewing the outcome of the war as a defeat of the forces of good at the heads of the powers of evil, the religious right has enshrouded itself within the American myth of origin. The Soviet Union is seen as a supernaturally evil entity which must be defeated by the United States—God's Kingdom—in an apocalyptic drama. But this false mythology, unmasked by the Vietnam experience, is certain to prove once again its utter moral and religious bankruptcy. Reflecting on Vietnam might provide some insights into the religious underpinnings which seem always to lock us into paths leading to disaster.

Taylor Stevenson diagnoses the nature of the Vietnam wound as "defilement"; i.e., coming into contact with an object which "has been culturally designated as being unclean" ("The Experience of Defilement," *Anglican Theological Review* [January 1982], p.18). That there is a good bit of truth in this assessment is demonstrated by the curious fact that many Vietnam veterans describe themselves as unclean. They lament the absence (or, in the case of the recent Washington observance, the delay) of the cleansing rituals of return, such as parades or a hero's welcome, that a society usually grants to its warriors. The almost total inability both of veterans and of the American public to discuss Vietnam for so many years is a clear indication of defilement. Stevenson sees this defilement as resulting from the breaking of two prerational taboos. These two sacred beliefs are part of American civil religion: (1) America is innocent, and (2) America is powerful. Stevenson writes:

> *America is innocent/powerful.* It is an implication of this innocency that America deserves to be peaceful and prosperous. A further implication here is that America's exercise of power is an innocent exercise of power necessary for our peace and prosperity. We were not "taught" this in any formal sense. It was not necessary to be taught this because this innocency is not a matter of idea or concept or doctrine; rather, it is a part of the texture of growing up in the United States. It is part of our story of how things *are*, how reality is structured, how life flows for us, and so on. Any violation of this asserted innocency is profoundly disturbing to our individual and social sense of structure and power....
>
> What breaks this taboo and brings a sense of defilement? Any situation or event which challenges or defeats the taboo and all that the taboo protects. Did we go into Vietnam originally under the taboo "America is innocent?" The evidence is overwhelming that, for the vast majority of Americans, we did (whatever reservations some had concerning Asian land wars).

Those on both sides of the Vietnam conflict were exposed to and participated in consciousness-altering, irreversible, massive evil. Atrocity, hatred, wholesale slaughter and barbarous acts of all kinds are the stuff of war. In the name of innocent America and its god, the GIs performed their duty in the great cultic act of war. But the myth was shattered. Neither they nor their country and its god were innocent. Perhaps, had the wages of sin been victory, a belief in our innocence could have been restored; but we were defeated. The other illusion, that of power, was also shattered. The warriors, their nation and its god were shown to be powerless. The taboos had been broken. We had sinned, and the wages of sin was death. Only in this context can the pervasive loss of faith among the veterans be understood and discussed.

Innocence Destroyed

What is most clear to me now is that I knew and understood all the political issues of the time. I saw why we were there and what we were doing, and why I should do my part. And at the foundation of my understanding was trust. I trusted and believed in the essential goodness of our leaders, and in the correctness of their perceptions. There was a deeply rooted belief in me that my country was not capable of doing evil in the world. The Vietnam experience has affected us all in many ways, and the most significant has been the profound change in that belief. . . .

I came to the certain knowledge that my country was capable of doing folly, that we Americans have the capacity to do evil in the world.

James N. Kennedy, letter, *Los Angeles Times*, October 1, 1983.

If, as John Wheeler writes, "God acting about us and through us redeems the brokenness of Vietnam" ("A Theological Reflection Upon the Vietnam War," *Anglican Theological Review* [January 1982], p.14), then this God can only be the God revealed to us in the Hebrew and Christian Scriptures. The veteran who told me that 500 years of life would not be sufficient to atone for what he did in Vietnam is quite correct, for those he killed would still be dead. Only death will erase the emotional and spiritual scars inflicted upon the widows and orphans of his victims. The veteran who asked me, "Where was God...when the rounds were coming in at Khe Sanh?" asked the right question. The mystery of iniquity is too profound for the American tribal god. Religious conservatives who retreat from evil and identify religion with feeling good about Jesus, with the conversion experience and with the better life are not really prepared to grapple with the questions raised by war. Neither are the liberals who believe that personhood and human fulfillment are the end products of religion. The former construct religious and emotional defenses to insulate themselves from evil, and the latter often underestimate its power....

Dealing with the Evil of Vietnam

For post-Christian vets, those whose faith was destroyed by Vietnam, I believe the most powerful single utterance in Scripture is the utterance of Jesus on the cross: "My God, my God, why have you abandoned me?" Quite clearly, they too have walked the way of the cross, and the words of the psalmist are their words too. The tragedy is that no one has pointed out this connection. Nor has anyone dealt with the next and crucial step that must be taken by those who have experienced great evil and perceived its relationship to the cross. With Jesus, one must be able to say, "Father, into your hands I commend my spirit." All that has happened to the veterans in Vietnam and since Vietnam—their broken lives, broken bodies and shattered dreams—must be placed in the hands of the Father. Experiential knowledge of the monstrous evil in the world and the recognition of humankind's utter inability to achieve any real shalom elicit the cry of agony. The next step requires the leap of faith, for the experience of evil is really the perception of God's absence from the world precisely in those situations which seem to demand a providential presence. To understand the apparent absence of God as one mode of his presence requires, first of all, the destruction of the American graven image, with its promise of innocence restored and power regained.

In more than ten years of working with Vietnam veterans, I have seen many discover the true nature of their wound. Although therapy, jobs and benefits may be helpful in healing some of the hurt, the real source of the alienation and rage is gradually disclosed: it is the death of the national god. For many veterans this abyss is too deep. To survive they must rewrite the history of Vietnam in their own minds and hearts. Beating the drums of war again seems the only way to justify their own war. For others, a life of service to fellow veterans and to society is the way to overcome the evil they have experienced. The enormous dedication and selflessness shown by those in the self-help centers, in the outreach programs and in the political groups can be explained in terms of deliverance from evil. Some even articulate their ideals in religious terms: the Beatitudes and the prayer of St. Francis....

The Vietnam experience has not yet been publicly connected with the dark night of the soul or with any theology of the cross. Yet I am aware of no other Christian point of reference adequate to it. Everything else "don't mean nothin'."

"What impresses me most about the vets I know is the sensibility that has emerged among them in recent years: a particular kind of moral seriousness which is unusual in America."

The War Developed Moral Sensitivity

Peter Marin

Peter Marin is a writer and a teacher. Shortly before writing the article from which this viewpoint is excerpted, he attended the first New York state convention of the Vietnam Veterans of America. He was greatly impressed with the sensitivity and generosity of the people he met there. In this viewpoint he describes the sense of moral complexity which the vets have developed and from which he believes the nation can learn.

As you read, consider the following questions:

1. What does the author mean by "the orphan effect"?
2. Why does Mr. Marin believe that the Vietnam war had a greater psychological impact on the participants than did earlier wars?
3. Why does Mr. Marin fear that the moral depth the veterans have developed may go to waste?

Peter Marin, "What the Vietnam Vets Can Teach Us," *The Nation*, November 27, 1982. *The Nation Magazine*, Nation Associates Incorporated © 1978.

What impresses me most about the vets I know is the sensibility that has emerged among them in recent years: a particular kind of moral seriousness which is unusual in America, one which is deepened and defined by the fact that it has emerged from a direct confrontation not only with the capacity of others for violence and brutality but also with their own culpability, their sense of their own capacity for error and excess. Precisely the same kinds of experiences that have produced in some vets the complex constellations of panic from which they seem unable to recover have engendered in others an awareness of moral complexity and human tragedy unlike anything one is likely to find elsewhere in America today....

These are vets who have, quite literally, brought one another back from the dead, often saved one another from suicide. Their relationships are full of a tenderness and generosity that is rare among American men—at least in public. (Sometimes they themselves are blissfully unaware of it; at others, when they notice it, they seem astonished.) I cannot remember seeing anything like it save among black college students in the late 1960s or among civil rights workers and elderly blacks in the South or—oddly enough—among the members of a fraternity to which I belonged in the 1950s, who seemed, beyond all rhetoric, to be genuinely brotherly toward one another.

It is this capacity for generosity, this kind of learned concern, which colors their moral sensibility, as if there were still at work in them a moral yearning or innocence that had somehow been deepened, rather than destroyed, by the war. A few days after I came home from my stay with the vets, a friend asked me: "Well, what is it they really want?" And I said, without thinking, "Justice." That is what they want, but it is not justice for themselves—though they would like that too. They simply want justice to *exist*, for there to be justice in the world: some moral order, a moral order maintained by other men and women one can trust. Their yearning is made all the more poignant by the fact that they still do not understand that if justice is to exist, they will have to be the ones who *create* rather than receive it. They do not yet—not *yet*—see it as their own work, not because they are lazy, but simply because it is not a role they associate with themselves. Like most Americans, they do not have a sense of themselves as makers and sustainers of moral values, even though, without knowing it, that is what many of them have become. . . .

Belief and Disillusionment

It is, paradoxically, the vets' yearning for goodness, for something to believe, which fuels their desire for justice but also makes them vulnerable to rhetoric and ritual, just as it did long ago when they went off to war.

One must remember: these were the good children. Several of them had fathers who served in World War II and passed on to them a sense of obligation and a belief in the glory of war. Many others—a surprising number, in fact—were Catholics who were inspired at an early age by John Kennedy's call to "ask what you can do for your country"; in fighting Communism (one must not forget how rigorously at the time American Catholicism was intent on confronting Communism everywhere), they would satisfy not only their parents, teachers and priests but also God and the Pope and the President—all at once. They were, in short, those whose faith in their elders, and in American myths and the American order of things, was so strong, so innocent, that war seemed beyond all doubt a good thing, a form of virtue.

Transforming Experience

No greater moral crime has been committed by the critics of the Vietnam War than to depersonalize and discredit the profound personal, transforming experience of the combat veteran. . . .

Whether the American wars of this century were a waste because politicians made them so is really irrelevant. Their meaning and significance for the surviving veteran is that when faced with the most personal, intense experience of his entire life he met the test and became part of the Brotherhood of the Brave.

Jeffrey St. John, *Conservative Digest*, December 1982.

And largely because their belief was so strong at the start—not only in the war but in all authority—their disillusionment and subsequent sense of loss were much stronger. One is tempted to call this an "orphan effect." They were cut off from any sustaining world. Church, state, parents, politicians, Army officers—all the hierarchical sources of moral truth and authority dissolved around them during the war, leaving them exposed without consolation to the stark facts of human culpability and brutality. I remember a remark I heard a vet make a year or two ago. He had said that he wondered if the Vietnamese people would ever forgive him for what he did. When someone asked whether he worried about God forgiving him, he answered, "*My* problem is that I haven't yet learned how to forgive *God*."

Effects of Vietnam

When I am asked, as I often am, why the Vietnam War so much affected—and so adversely affected—these young men, I am always surprised by the question, because the answers seem to me so obvious.

In the first place, it is probable that all wars have devastating effects upon the men they use—and these were not men when they fought but adolescents, averaging just about 19 years of age. It is hard to believe that something similar to what the soldiers in Vietnam felt was not felt by the men involved in the pointless horrors of trench warfare in World War I; and I cannot help thinking about what one vet told me in Rochester about his father and World War II:

"He never talked much about it except for the usual glorious things, about service to the country and becoming a man. But every year, on New Year's Day, he would lock himself into his den and get dead drunk. He never explained why he did it, but I think now he was remembering the war and mourning. Once, just once, after I got back from Nam, he asked me what it was like, and then he began talking about his war and what he had seen and how it had felt, the killing and the death, and he didn't really feel very much different about it than I did about Nam. It was simply that he had kept it to himself."

For another thing, although what happened to many men in Vietnam did happen to other men in other wars, the cumulative psychological effects were much greater. War, to be sure, is hell, but the effects of this one were compounded by its specific characteristics, as witnessed by the fact that a higher percentage of veterans emerged from this war with psychological disturbances than, as far as we know, from any previous war. (Without question, the rate of suicide and attempted suicide is higher among Vietnam vets than among those of other wars.) Moreover, the attention paid to the damages wrought upon the veterans by this war has been much greater than in the past.

A Bad War

There are other elements that make the Vietnam War different from and even worse than other wars. Even now most Americans do not realize the extent to which it was marked by arbitrary killing and the murder of civilians—out of either official policy or the casual, recreational or simply half-mad behavior of individual men apparently subject to neither internal nor external constraint. It was a war in which innocents became fair game and in which our soldiers—who went to war convinced they were saviors and guardians of freedom—found themselves perceived by the civilian population as intruders, conquerers and even murderers. Their military leaders at several levels of command proved to be venal, dishonest or stupid, and everywhere around them flourished forms of American corruption and vice—black-marketeering, profiteering, thievery—which most of them had never seen close up before. It was a bad war fought for all the wrong reasons and in all the wrong ways, and one could hardly avoid seeing that after being in it for a short while. All of the death, and all of the risk, and even all of the camaraderie and bravery that mark the lives of soldiers anywhere, even those engaged in wrong causes—all of that was rendered meaningless and unnecessary because the war itself was so obviously a bad one.

And there is, finally, one other reason for the Vietnam vets' special pain: we have, as a people, and largely without knowing it, shifted our attitudes toward war, outgrowing the ease with which we may once have accepted violence. Cultures *do* grow up; just as certain moral attitudes can atrophy, others can develop. Many Americans are no longer able to accept without queston or horror the nature of war; indeed, it may well be that in future wars (save for the most obviously self-defensive) many combatants will feel, afterward, what the vets now feel about Vietnam. In short, the vets may be experiencing, as their *individual* pain, the half-conscious tensions and confusions that Americans, as a society, now bring to violence and war.

Commitment and Love

And so there grew up in Vietnam combat units a sense of commitment and love among the men who lived, laughed, suffered and died together. You took your turn on point, pushing into the terrible unknown of the jungle or down an exposed rice-paddy dike, you went up a hill under fire, you crawled out after the wounded—not for your country: you did it for your buddies.

William Broyles Jr., *Newsweek*, November 22, 1982.

Therefore, more than veterans of any other wars past, what these men have been forced to confront is *their own capacity for error*; they understand that whatever they experienced—the horror, the terror—has its roots and complements in their own weaknesses and mistakes. For them, all conversation about human error or evil is a conversation about themselves; they are pushed past smug ideology and the condemnation of others to an examination of the world that is an examination of self. They know there is no easy relation between one's self-image and the consequences of one's actions. They know too that whatever truths one holds at any given moment will turn out to be if not mistaken then at least incomplete, and that often one's opponents or antagonists will turn out to have been more right than one thought and probably as serious in intention as oneself. Because they cannot easily divide the world into two camps, and because they cannot easily claim virtue while ascribing evil to others, they inhabit a moral realm more complex than the one in which most others live. They know that a moral life means an acknowledgment of guilt as well as a claim to virtue, and they have learned—oh, hardest lesson of all—to judge their own actions in terms of their irrevocable consequences to others....

Wasteful Isolation

But this moral depth, this seriousness, may well go to waste—that is what is most poignant about it. The vets for the most part remain so isolated, so locked into their own pain, that there are few avenues for what is within them to make its way into the larger world or be sustained and referred by the larger world. If someone somewhere would take the trouble to draw forth from the veterans what it is they feel, think and know, or to convince them to speak, all of us would be better off.

It is probably true, as Karl Jaspers pointed out almost four decades ago in talking to the German people about guilt, that people can look closely at their own moral guilt only when others around them are willing to consider *their* lives in the same way. This is precisely what the vets have been denied, and therefore their seriousness—which ought to afford them entrance into the larger world, connecting them to all those others who have thought about and suffered similar things—does not. They cannot locate men or women willing to take them as seriously as they take the questions that plague them.

That is what seems so wasteful, and there is something almost unforgivable about it. I have seen similar kinds of waste over and over in America during the past several decades: among children, whose sense of community and fair play is allowed to atrophy or is conscientiously discouraged; in universities, where the best and deepest yearnings of students go unacknowledged or untapped; even in literature, where, with very few exceptions, the capacities for generosity and concern which abound unrecognized in most men and women have gone unexamined. But for this to happen to the vets is perhaps the greatest waste of all, since, in many of them, so much understanding has so obviously emerged from their experience....

Coming to Terms

The vets' difficulty in coming to terms with their own past, coupled with their refusal to put it aside, their stubbornness in clinging to its inchoate power, is not very different from the even more hidden yearnings and sorrows of many Americans about many things—yearnings for which we no longer have a usable language, and which no longer form (as they once would have) the center of our conversations about what it means to be human.

What is more, the vets' loss of the myths that ordinarily protect people from the truth has brought them face to face with several problems that beleaguer almost all those who approach value from a secular position: the difficulty of dealing with questions of good and evil in the absence of divine, absolute and binding powers or systems. We have learned by now—or we should have—that humans kill just as easily in God's absence as they do in his name, and that the secularization of values, which people believed a hundred years ago might set them free of ignorance and superstition, leads along its own paths to ignorance and superstition. To be absolutely honest, *none* of us who are secular thinkers have anything more than the tatters of past certainty to offer in regard to establishing and sustaining morality, or increasing kindness in men and women and justice in the world. These questions, which plague the vets, ought to plague every thinking man and woman, and none of us can afford to ignore the vets' experience.

In the end, what we owe the dead (whether our own or the Vietnamese), what we owe the vets and what we owe ourselves is the same thing: the resumption of the recurrent conversation about moral values, the sources and meaning of conscience, and the roots of human generosity, solidarity and community.

"A three-year study of the war's after-effects says that P.T.S.D. afflicts 500,000 of Vietnam's combat veterans."

Post-War Stress Is Afflicting Veterans

Philip Caputo

Philip Caputo is a veteran of Vietnam and a writer. His book *A Rumor of War* is one of the most acclaimed personal accounts of the Vietnam experience. He recently published his second novel, *DelCorso's Gallery*, about a combat photographer. In the following viewpoint Mr. Caputo discusses Post Traumatic Stress Disorder, a severe, *delayed*, psychological reaction suffered by many Vietnam veterans.

As you read, consider the following questions:

1. How does the author say that P.T.S.D. differs from the "shell shock" suffered by the veterans of earlier wars?
2. What are the symptoms of P.T.S.D.?
3. What does Mr. Caputo see as a remedy for P.T.S.D.?

It seems fitting for a war that gave the world such arcana as "protective reaction air strike" to hand us a phrase like post-traumatic stress disorder to describe what was known in the World Wars and Korea as shell shock or battle fatigue. The symptoms are much the same, with this difference: Battle fatigue occurred most often in combat or soon afterward; the symptoms of P.T.S.D. are showing up five, ten and as many as 15 years after the soldier has come home. Every now and then, we read about some French farmer, plowing the fields of Verdun, getting blown up by an unexploded mine or shell that has been buried for decades. Something like that is happening in the minds of Vietnam veterans: experiences and emotions long repressed are detonating unexpectedly, frequently with catastrophic results....

It's a big army, this legion of men with hidden wounds. Dr. John P. Wilson, a Cleveland State University psychologist who recently completed a three-year study of the war's aftereffects, says that P.T.S.D. afflicts 500,000 of Vietnam's combat veterans. Other researchers put the number at 700,000 which would give a psychiatric casualty rate among combatants of 50 to 70 percent. (Only 1,100,000 of the 2,800,000 men who served in the war saw action.)

Reversion to Warrior

"The combat veteran has a higher level of stress," Wilson tells me in an interview. "Most of these men have repressed the Vietnam experience for so long that it's become an integral part of their personalities. They are in a constant state of stress. Daily stresses they might have been able to cope with—a divorce, or losing a job, or not having enough money, or problems with the kids—may push them beyond their threshold. They become fully symptomatic. They revert back to the warrior."

"Fully symptomatic" means the veteran manifests several of the 25 major signs of posttraumatic stress disorder. Those include prolonged spells of depression or anxiety, outbursts of apparently senseless rage, chronic insomnia, war nightmares, emotional distancing from children, wife or other loved ones, intrusive, obsessive memories of a war experience and flashbacks—hallucinatory re-creations of the battlefield. Although P.T.S.D. can degenerate into actual psychosis, Wilson and clinical psychologist Dr. Charles Figley of Purdue University (a Marine enlisted man in Vietnam) emphasize that the condition is untraditional as psychological disorders go; for example, it doesn't relate back to the formative years of a person's personality but is, rather, a reaction to the extreme stress of combat....

What made Vietnam so different that anywhere from half to three fourths of its combat veterans are, to varying degrees, going haywire? War is war, after all. Getting shot at wasn't any less unpleasant in Belleau Wood or at Normandy or on the Pusan perimeter than it was in Khe Sanh, Hue or the Iron Triangle. Nevertheless, Vietnam was like no other conflict Americans have fought.

Being There

You had to have been there to know what it was like, patrolling in those jungles, swamps and rice paddies, mud up to your ass, leeches doing their Dracula act on you, mosquitoes pumping you full of malaria, wet leaves caressing your face, and the trails winding off into nowhere, the point man looking for trip wires and ambushes, and the thick silence suddenly broken by an explosion, the point man's on his way home, maybe in pieces, maybe with his legs or his testicles gone. You had to have spent a few nights on perimeter watch at some fire base, waiting for the mortars to start falling, waiting for silence, yes, silence, waiting for the frogs and crickets and other creepy crawlies out there in the malarial slime to stop croaking and chirping, because when they did it, it meant an infiltrator was slithering toward you, and then—crack-crack-crack—the infiltrator lets off a few rounds, but you don't know if

Reprinted by permission of Newspaper Enterprise Association.

he's some lone, gung-ho Charley looking for the V.C. equivalent of a Congressional Medal of Honor or the point man for a whole battalion massing in the blood-black darkness for a rush at the wire. And if it wasn't a patrol or a perimeter watch, it was a C.A.—combat assault—and, sweet Jesus, that could be something, swooping down a roller coaster with no up to it, the door gunner's

M-60 spitting brass cartridges 700 a minute, the antiaircraft fire going pop-pop-pop so that you thought you were trapped in some kind of huge, lethal popcorn machine, down and down, the green paddies rushing up at you, green flecked with the gray of bursting mortars, down into the crackling, thudding chaos of a hot LZ.

And if you were a grunt, you did this all the time. You stayed in the bush your whole tour except for a five-day clap-catching expedition to Bangkok or Hong Kong—R & R they called it. The rest of the time, you were in combat. Here's a comparison for you: The Sixth Marines, the regiment Leon Uris wrote about in Battle Cry, spent only six weeks of its four years in the South Pacific fighting Japanese. Constant service at the front made Vietnam a very lethal war for combat outfits. The Marines suffered more casualties in Indochina than in World War Two, about 102,000 dead and wounded, as compared with 87,000.

The bloodshed would have been tolerable if it had accomplished something. In a conventional army, progress is measured by seizing hills or towns or road junctions. You take this place, move on and take the next place, and the more places you take, the closer you are to victory. MacArthur was right: There is no substitute for victory, because, to the combat soldier, the drive toward victory symbolizes commitment, tells him that the hell he's going through is for something. In Vietnam, the only measure of victory was one of the most hideous, morally corrupting ideas ever conceived by the military mind—the body count. You fought over the same ground again and again, month after month, your only object to kill more of them than they did of you. In 1972, I read an account of a patrol from the 28th Infantry, one of the last line outfits to fight in the war. The patrol suffered two casualties in a fire fight outside a village where I had been in my first fire fight—in 1965. Put it this way: When I got into my scrap, the troopers in that patrol were in seventh grade. It was a long war.

A Young War

It was also a young one, literally a case of sending boys to do a man's job. Most of the soldiers who went there probably carried Clearasil in their duffel bags. The average age of the World War Two soldier was 26; in Vietnam, it was 19, an age at which youth is barely equipped to deal with the ups and downs of ordinary life, let alone the incredible stresses of the battlefield.

Finally, it was a guerrilla war, which meant you couldn't tell the good guys (and girls) from the bad guys (and girls), unless you were fighting North Vietnamese regulars. You could tell only when they shot at you, and then it was too late. That did two things to the American fighting man: It knocked his ideological pins out from under him; most went to war believing they were going to help save the Vietnamese and stop communism, but their experience made it impossible to maintain that conviction. The Vietnamese whom they thought they were saving turned out to be indifferent to salvation, American style; and if they weren't indifferent, they were hostile. Lacking a clear demarcation between who was enemy and who was friend, the fighting man became suspicious of all Vietnamese, women and children included. The war was totally unpredictable and treacherous; the soldier had no idea who was going to try to kill him, had no idea if an ambush or booby trap or sniper was waiting for him in that "friendly" village down the trail. This condition eventually induced a kind of paranoia and even a hatred for the very people he had initially wanted to save. All he wanted to do was save himself, to survive. And when you're faced with a choice between survival and death or maiming, you are apt to do some things the folks back home won't want to hear about....

Isolated Vets

"Lots of Vietnam vets ostensibly living within society are extremely isolated," reports psychologist Stephen Silver of the Veterans Hospital in Coatesville, Pa. "I've treated guys who've had 60 jobs in 12 or 15 years, who never live in one place more than three or four months, who take jobs as nightwatchmen so they never have to deal with people. These kinds of folks are just as isolated as a guy on a mountain someplace.

Joanne Davidson & John S. Lang, *U.S. News & World Report*, March 12, 1984.

Even primitive cultures recognize that war is not a natural condition, that evil spirits enter the warrior in battle. That is why these cultures, such as the Navaho Indians, perform elaborate purification rites for the returning warrior. His soul is cleansed, his feats of arms are passed into tribal lore, he is accepted back into the tribe and forgiven whatever taboos he may have broken in the crisis of combat. In modern society, these rites often take the form of welcoming ceremonies, patriotic speeches, tickertape parades with bands and flags and bunting. The veteran is given first choice in the job market, lavished with benefits such as the generous GI Bill afforded the men who fought in World War Two. In psychologist Wilson's words, "These are signs of a societal commitment, signs that your country was behind you."

The Vietnam veteran returned to find that the country was not only not behind him, it was at best indifferent to him, at worst against him. Flown in a jet plane that took him from the front line to his front porch in only 48 hours, leaving him no time to make sense out of what he'd been through, he was ignored by the mainstream of American society, stigmatized by the liberal left and by the media as a dope-crazed killer, an accomplice of a criminal foreign policy. And he lost whatever shreds of faith he had left, shrank into himself, refused to talk about his feelings and experiences, repressed powerful, unresolved emotions. Johnny didn't come marching home from Vietnam; he crept back, furtive, secretive and alone, like a convict just released from prison.

"Vietnam veterans were stigmatized as villains, so they held everything in," Wilson says. "But carrying a problem around is a stress in itself. It must be talked out or acted out eventually."

A Triple Burden of Guilt

If my own postwar experience and those of other veterans I've talked to are typical, the main unresolved problem is guilt, a triple burden of guilt. There is the guilt all soldiers feel for having broken the taboo against killing, a guilt as old as war itself....

Add to this the soldier's sense of shame for having fought in actions that resulted, indirectly or directly, in the deaths of civilians. Then pile on top of that an attitude that made the fighting men feel personally morally responsible for the war, and you get your proverbial walking time bomb. Wilson has noted that some of the crimes committed by Vietnam veterans are violent, hideously violent. Because these men were never allowed to remove the taint some are trying, through commission of terrible acts, to call attention to the evil they perceive in themselves and force society to punish them.

That isn't all. The Yanks came home in World War Two to a generous GI Bill that went a long way toward helping them adjust to civilian life. Lyndon Johnson tried to veto the bill's educational benefits, then reintroduced it under pressure in 1966. In 1972, Richard Nixon successfully vetoed the Veterans Health Care Expansion Act; he said the act was fiscally irresponsible and inflationary, an interesting claim to make at a time when the U.S. was still spending billions to blow Vietnam to bits with B-52s and poison its forests with Agent Orange. And in his initial cost-cutting efforts, David Stockman, President Reagan's budget wizard, wanted to cut out the Veterans Administration Readjustment Counseling Program for Veterans of the Vietnam Era. He argued that it was inflationary, though spending more billions on a fleet of block-long carriers and squadrons of Buck Rogers bombers was not. Bowing to pressure from Vietnam veterans' organizations, the Administration finally decided to leave the program alone—for now.

Inadequate Benefits

And if there ever was a generation of American soldiers that needed adequate benefits, the Vietnam generation was it. America sent its most poorly educated sons to Indochina, dug them out of the basement levels of society and gave them rifles, while the privileged bought tickets to Toronto or hid in the bunkers of student deferments. With no marketable skills and a couple of years of high school, thousands of Vietnam veterans returned to an economy that combined inflation with a tight job market; they went from the firing line to the unemployment line, and the Government's tightwad attitude toward them was another sign that society regarded them as outcasts....

Conclusion

If America wants its Vietnam veterans to be cleansed, if it wants them to come home, it must give them genuine compassion, dignity and respect: compassion for having been misused, dignity for having answered the call to arms and doing their duty as they saw it, respect for having had the courage and tenacity to survive.

"The modern concept of 'delayed stress' allows the government that devised war policy to block out the social and political history of the war among veterans and those who attempt to help them."

Post-War Stress Is Exaggerated

Clark Smith

Clark Smith is a director of the Winter Soldier Archive as well as the author of *The Vietnam Map Book: A Self-Help Guide to Herbicide Exposure* and *Brothers: Black Soldiers in the Nam, An Oral History.* In the following viewpoint, excerpted from a longer article about Vietnam veteran concerns, he points out that the Vietnam vet does indeed suffer from after-effects of the war. But, he says, the idea of post-traumatic stress disorder is being used to distract the public from the real issues and problems of the veteran.

As you read, consider the following questions:

1. The author believes that far fewer veterans suffer from actual P.T.S.D. than is commonly stated. Instead, what does he believe most of them *do* suffer?
2. In what sense does Mr. Smith believe that P.T.S.D. is an isolating factor for vets?
3. In what ways does he believe that P.T.S.D. has been politicized?

Clark Smith, "The Soldier-Cynics: Veterans Still Caught in a War," *Southeast Asia Chronicle,* Issue No. 85, August 1982.

The veteran of the war came home encapsulated in cynicism, tortured by anger, grieving for lost friends. He confronted a sometimes hostile, sometimes indifferent, usually uncomprehending community of family, friends, and acquaintances. On his way home, as a final statement of his alienation and disgust, he discarded the outward manifestation of his military identity. As former Specialist 4 John Imsdahl, also of the 101st Airborne, commented on his arrival with a busload of Vietnam veterans going home:

> We all climbed on the buses they had waiting and they sent us to Seattle-Tacoma Airport. When we got there, everybody got off that damned bus and beelined it for the men's room. I was in the second bus. By the time I got there, there was forty uniforms stuffed in the urinals and toilets with Silver Stars on them, Purple Hearts. It didn't matter. New Class-A uniforms stuffed in garbage cans—all dumped for civilian clothes.

But the shedding of the uniform could not immediately eliminate the military identity. The experience remained. Only the veteran professionalized in his Vietnam service of the "early war" of late 1965 and 1966 was likely to be reprieved from these attitudes.

Alienated Vets

Veterans came home to watch the war on television—certainly a first in American veteran history. What they so often saw was in conflict with what they experienced, which sharpened their cynicism. They remained caught, too, between a government forced to defend bankrupt war policies and a public outraged or confused by the war. The My Lai exposure riveted attention on present and former soldiers alike.... Though a small but vocal group of veterans was able to vent its anger against the war, most merely hid. Former Sergeant Ernie Boitano, 3rd of the 47 Mobile Riverines, describes his reaction:

> We were alienated by our peers—the people we were going to end up associating with back in the States, back in the world. We felt lost. From '68 to '70 there was such a big transition in social consciousness in the United States. People were saying, "What the hell are we doing [in Vietnam]? Then all of a sudden people were saying things like, "The guys coming back from Vietnam ought to be put in detention camps." I can't remember whether it was *Newsweek* where there was talk about doing psychoanalysis to make sure they could adjust Vietnam veterans so they could fit back into society. All I wanted to do was pull a blanket over my head and go through everything incognito. For the most part, vets would not talk to anybody about what happened....

Post-Traumatic Stress Disorder

"Stress" is very much in vogue these days and it has swallowed the veteran whole. Though there is no doubt that the variations of stress among Vietnam veterans are profound and continuing, psychologists found it a readily adaptable term to cover a wide range of emotional states. Initially, "Post-Vietnam Syndrome" defined the clinical state of the veteran's psyche. It was a term accepted by many veterans which defined their anger and frustration, but also housed anti-war attitudes among those fresh from the Vietnam combat zone. These attitudes were a mixture of anger against the brass for incompetence and self-serving ambitions, against Washington politicians who made or supported war policies, and against even the economic structure which benefited from the war, but it was also against war protestors who manifested ultra-radical sympathies but had escaped the war experience. As the anti-war movement faded at war's end, psychologists discovered "Post Traumatic Stress Disorder," attributable in some undefined sense to all Vietnam veterans. This concept implied a fundamental notion: everyone could forget the war except the veteran who remained in a state of unresolved emotional conflict. This emotional distress was noted for its "delayed" response, said psychologists anxious to promote a psychiatric solution to the problems faced by Vietnam veterans. And, in some cases—stripped of its political character—"delayed stress" does occur when a veteran manifests unexpressed feelings about the war.

Adjusted Vets

"The time has come for the public to be made aware that many of us [Vietnam Veterans] are much more successful socially, politically and economically than the derelict so often stereotyped by the media," comments William C. Stensland, a former marine who heads a veterans' program in Texas.

"It is very important to recognize that more than 80 percent of the Vietnam veterans, even with enormous difficulties, have come home and made the successful transition to civilian life," asserts Thomas W. Pauken, an Army veteran who heads the federal ACTION program.

Wendell S. Merrick, *U.S. News & World Report*, March 29, 1982.

Casual events might trigger the "delayed stress" syndrome. Take an extreme case: A veteran lives near a church. On Sunday parishioners routinely arrive and depart with much slamming of car doors. From inside his apartment, the repeated door slamming reverberates on a subconscious conditioned at an earlier time to an identical sound, the initial thud of a mortar round leaving its tube—a threatening anticipation of death or dismemberment. If the veteran is sufficiently in touch with the source of increasing anxiety, he moves to less stressful surroundings; if not (as in the case above), the pressure increases. The apprehension and anxiety arouses old fears in the daytime, renewed nightmares in sleep. Finally, the veteran snaps. The aggression that is released is either externalized in anti-social behavior or is internalized in suicide or one of its substitutes (alcohol or drug abuse). But this example does not fit most veterans, though television dramas often create and maintain such a caricature.

Post Traumatic Stress Disorder is a problematic concept, because it draws all Vietnam veterans within its sweep yet truly applies to only very few if it means sudden and unexplained stress resulting from renewed confrontation with the war experience. For many thousands of Vietnam veterans stress has not been "delayed"; rather it has *continued* from the time they left Vietnam until the present. Likewise, Vietnam-related stress need not be traumatic. On those occasions when stress leads to trauma, the delay is only in the psychiatric recognition. But an enduring, non-traumatic "stress" is the description that best fits Vietnam veterans and it is akin to cynicism rather than psychological illness. Such stress as there is is drawn from the emotional despair to find a rationalization of war experiences under the impact of the My Lai accusation. Or it is focused on the desire to see the real perpetrators of the war policies punished. It represents attitudes shared by many non-veterans. It is unlikely that psychological counseling under the rubric of "delayed stress" can counter the widespread cynicism of veterans that fits the realization that they were, *in fact* betrayed by country and commanders. The "delayed stress" notion only further isolates the veteran and therefore has the effect of a political tactic.

Prejudicial Labels

It is certainly small comfort to the soldier-cynic that memory of the Vietnam War is defined in clinical terms. In attempting to assist a small minority of Vietnam veterans in emotional conflict, psychologists have sought to depoliticize the war. Instead of reinforcing the significant, honest insights into the politics of the war, they have made the Vietnam veteran *en masse* into a psychiatric "case." Not only does the concept of "delayed stress" prove overly elastic, but it also serves nicely to deflect the powerful political energies of Vietnam veterans against the war. After all, Colonel Haig became General Haig and then Secretary of State Haig; junior officers of the Vietnam War became senior officers of the post-war period. If names like Rusk, McNamara, Lyndon Johnson and Nixon are gone, those that replaced them certainly traveled on the path they made. But veterans in general remained labeled as psychiatric misfits and social pariahs. All of the forces that created the Vietnam War remain in place and most veterans have not forgotten it. So the notion of stress as conceived by a few psychologists fits nicely with the data from former President Ford that Americans should forget the war, that it was a "mistake" not to be considered in future political deliberations. Therefore, by implication, the veterans can be forgotten. The modern concept of "delayed stress" allows the government that devised war policy to block out the social and political history of the war among veterans and those who attempt to help them.

PTSD as Political Tactic

One of the interesting side effects of the promotion of "delayed stress" has been its use by the Veterans Administration. Veterans who have appeared for screening of possible herbicide exposure in the wake of revelations about Agent Orange have been categorized as victims of "stress.". . .

Just how many veterans have died of cancer, fathered defective children or remain captive to complicated and untreatable symptoms is not known. What is clear is that they bear an often invisible scar of the trauma of war—unseen mutagens which will be passed on to subsequent generations. That all of this is somehow reducible to "stress" is part of the politics of an unseen cluster of militarists in the Veterans Administration and the Department of Defense.

Probably no veterans of American wars have been so beset with problems as the Vietnam veteran. Renewed discussion of the Vietnam War, the recurring image of war in other countries seen on television, continuing and emerging health problems compounded by stress will continue to link him with his outworn military identity. Since retreat has not worked for the Vietnam veteran, some veterans have begun to gather together, usually informally, in small self-help groups. This seems a tentative step out of isolation and containment. Though veterans are scattered throughout society, transcending class and race, they have a common experience that was profoundly educational about the nature of their society. No one should expect them to forget it. A young lawyer, when asked why he wears his old military belt with his stylish three-piece suit, responded, "It gives me a sense of perspective."

117

Distinguishing Between Fact and Opinion

This activity is designed to help develop the basic reading and thinking skill of distinguishing between fact and opinion. Consider the following statement as an example. "The United States was militarily involved in Vietnam in 1970." This is a fact which no historian or diplomat would deny. But let us consider a statement which makes a judgment about US involvement in Vietnam. "The aggressive foreign policy of North Vietnam was a major cause of the Vietnam War." Such a statement is clearly an expressed opinion. Attributing blame concerning the cause of the war in Vietnam obviously depends upon one's point of view. A citizen of Vietnam will view the Vietnam War from a far different perspective than will a citizen of the United States.

When investigating controversial issues it is important that one be able to distinguish between statements of fact and statements of opinion.

Many of the following statements are taken from the viewpoints in this book. Some have other origins. Consider each statement carefully. *Mark O for any statement you feel is an opinion or interpretation of facts. Mark F for any statement you believe is a fact.*

Step 1.   After each individual in the class has ranked the statements below, break the class into small groups of four to six students. Students should compare their rankings with others in their group, giving the reasons for their rankings.

$$O = opinion$$
$$F = fact$$

1. The US tried to erect in South Vietnam a government which the people clearly resisted.

2. US policy in Vietnam was a tragic mistake.

3. The press was instinctively "agin the government"—and, at least reflexively, for Saigon's enemies.

4. A declaration of war is a clear statement of initial public support which focuses the nation's attention on the enemy.

5. It is vital to US interests to stop communist expansion wherever it occurs with whatever force is necessary.

6. President Johnson sent combat troops to Vietnam.

7. US military involvement in Vietnam was immoral.

8. The antiwar movement in the US during the Vietnam war was unpatriotic.

9. The US continues to pursue the same Communist containment policies elsewhere and endorses the same anti-communist tactics that failed in Vietnam.

10. Communism is a great threat to our well-being and security.

11. The USSR currently has military bases in Vietnam.

Step 2.   Each small group should write four statements which the group agrees are statements of fact. Write one statement on each of the following issues.
1.   The role and responsibility of communism for the war in Vietnam
2.   The role and responsibility of US political leaders for the US loss in Vietnam
3.   The morality of US involvement in Vietnam
4.   The consequences of the US loss in Vietnam for American society

Step 3.   Each small group should share its four statements of fact with the other small groups.

Periodical Bibliography

The following list of periodical articles deals with the subject matter of this chapter.

William Broyles Jr.	"Remembering a War We Want to Forget," *Newsweek*, November 22, 1982.
C.D.B. Bryan	"The Veterans' Ordeal," *The New Republic*, June 27, 1983.
Christopher Buckley	"Viet Guilt," *Esquire*, September 1983.
Milton R. Copulos	"Agent Orange: Resolving a Painful Vietnam War Legacy," *Backgrounder*, The Heritage Foundation, 214 Massachusetts Ave. NE, Washington, DC 20002.
James Fallows	"What Did You Do in the Class War, Daddy?" *The Washington Monthly*, October 1975.
Tony Fuller, and Richard Banning, et al.	"What Vietnam Did to Us," *Newsweek*, December 14, 1981.
Guenter Lewy	"Vietnam: New Light on the Question of American Guilt," *Commentary*, February 1978.
Doug Magee	"Vietnam: The Body Count Still Rises," *Christianity & Crisis*, October 5, 1981.
Peter Marin	"Living in Moral Pain," *Psychology Today*, November 1981.
Lewis M. Milford	"Justice Is Not a GI Benefit," *The Progressive*, August 1981.
Tom Morganthau, et, al.	"The Troubled Vietnam Vet," *Newsweek*, March 30, 1981.
Stephen J. Morris	"Vietnam Under Communism," *Commentary*, September 1982.
Timothy Noah	"The Vet Offensive (What Vietnam Vets Need and What They Don't), *The New Republic*, August 1/8, 1981.
Ginnetta Sagan	"Vietnam's Postwar Hell," *Newsweek*, May 3, 1982.
Jeffrey St. John	"A Question of Honor," *Conservative Digest*, December 1982.
USA Today	"Psychiatric Problems of Vietnam Veterans," August 1981.
Lawrence Walsh	"Vietnam for a Thousand Years?" *The Progressive*, December 1982.

What Are the Lessons of Vietnam?

"The United States continues to pursue the same Communist containment policies elsewhere and endorses the same anti-Communist tactics that failed in Vietnam."

The US Must Stop Cold War Posturing

Joseph A. Amter

Joseph A. Amter, a lawyer and banker, has had a life-long interest in foreign affairs and world peace. In 1962 he founded the Peace Research Organization Fund. He served under President Lyndon Johnson as co-chairman of the White House Conference on International Cooperation. The following viewpoint is taken from Mr. Amter's book, *Vietnam Verdict: A Citizen's History.* In this excerpt he discusses the folly of maintaining a containment policy in today's precarious world.

As you read, consider the following questions:

1. To what does the author attribute US involvement in Vietnam?
2. In the author's opinion, what impact does the CIA have on US foreign policy?
3. What conclusions does the author come to? Do you agree?

The United States lost the war in Vietnam, which has now become a Communist state. Yet the United States continues to pursue the same Communist containment policies elsewhere and endorses the same anti-Communist tactics that failed in Vietnam.

It is the American people rather than their government who have learned from the Vietnam experience. Many Americans today fear that Cold War policy as it was carried out in Vietnam will eventually lead to nuclear war. They are demanding a nuclear freeze, and politicians at all levels of American government are beginning to listen. If popular demand could break the pattern of nuclear escalation, it would surely be a giant step forward.

Yet even a freeze would not eliminate the terrible threat of nuclear holocaust. Everyone in the United States can be killed many times over with the nuclear weapons that already exist. The true road to a more stable international environment would be to combine a nuclear freeze with a freeze on Cold War propaganda. If we could shed the rigidity of Cold War anti-Communism, we could view the world in its great variety and create flexible approaches to world problems.

Some special-interest groups and individuals tell us that we must continue to wage the Cold War and, if necessary, a hot war that we make sure to win next time. In the 1950s when Cold War doctrine was being hammered out, one of its architects said, "If we can sell every useless article known to man in large quantities, we should be able to sell our very fine story in larger quantities." Using all the techniques of modern marketing, the Cold Warriors did succeed in selling us the Cold War.

The Cold War Story

Here is that lavishly financed story as we have heard it through the years:

> Because of the nature of Communism, the Soviet Union is determined to enslave its own people and its neighbors, and will then proceed to destroy America and enslave the world.
> Because Communists are fanatics willing to pour all their resources into world domination, the Soviets have drawn ahead of us in armaments. Therefore we Americans must devote more and more of our own money to the arms race.
> Because Communism is a super-secret, super-powerful worldwide movement, we must support our own Cold Warriors no matter what they do, even if they lie to us while doing it.

Those Cold Warriors who now control foreign policy in the United States do not appear to recognize the changes that make the 1980s different from the 1950s. It is important that the people of this country examine and debate whether or not in today's world the policies that led to Vietnam should be continued. It is the lives and well-being of the American people that are at stake, and it is imperative that *they* decide whether the trouble caused by the Cold War is still worth the price.

Slow learner

THE LESSONS OF VIETNAM

Reprinted with permission from the *Minneapolis Star and Tribune*.

All the formulas of Cold War strategy—subversion, puppet dictatorships, secret war, and, finally, open war—were methodically used in Vietnam. Despite the lives we sacrificed, the billions we spent, and the evil we did, our Vietnam involvement was a foreign policy disaster at every stage.

On balance, the Cold War has been a failure. It has not enabled us to eradicate Communism or destroy the Soviet Union. It has certainly not produced peace. It has led our government to interfere secretly in the affairs of Third World nations, to support and sometimes create corrupt dictatorships, to stockpile arms like a military state, and recklessly to escalate small wars that have nothing to do with us. Despite the incalculable cost of the efforts that the United States has made for decades to curtail Soviet power, the U.S. government now tells its citizens that the Soviet Union exceeds us in military strength and that, despite our own weakened economy, we must spend almost a trillion dollars in an arms race to catch up.

Many other Western nations, however, are convinced that the Soviet Union is no longer a major threat to the world, that the influence of the Soviets has declined, that their economy is in a shambles, that they desperately need peace in order to hold their own empire together, and that Communism has proved itself so ineffective that few want it except underdeveloped nations who have no other source of capital.

Why Containment Policy?

In order to end the Vietnam War, the United States ultimately acknowledged that it no longer had a real problem with Communism in the People's Republic of China. President Nixon negotiated a rapprochement with China and its one billion Communist citizens, and this country began the normalization of trade, travel, and other relations with them. In simple logic, why are we still pursuing the Communist containment policy against the Soviet Union? What differentiates Russian Communists from their Chinese counterparts?

It would appear that the Soviet Union has materially altered Stalin's old crusade to colonize the world, because the Soviets found this policy both expensive and counterproductive. They continue, however, to support groups in underdeveloped countries whom they hope will become their friends and whom they claim are trying to overthrow dictators supported by the United States. Certainly the Russians feel the need to counteract U.S. Cold War activities. By now it is difficult to know whether we act because of them or they act because of us and to determine which is the chicken and which the egg in any world trouble spot.

We have pointed out why it is necessary for the American people to discuss the need to curtail cold Warism as exemplified by Vietnam. There appears to be a reluctance by politicians and political leaders in the public sector to curtail Cold War activities. Why? Who benefits from the Cold War? Pentagon officials who need an enemy in order to increase their appropriations? Defense contractors who spend millions on Cold War propaganda? Politicians who rise to power by manipulating our love of America and fear of foreign interference? Right-wing Cold Warriors who have a phobic fear of Socialism and Communism? In any event, all these groups and many others exert pressure on the President to continue the Cold War. . . .

CIA Manipulation

Billions of U.S. dollars have been spent over the years in arming, supporting, and assisting anti-Communist governments and providing undisclosed funds to the CIA. The CIA was employed in Vietnam, Laos, and Cambodia for many years as a secret force for subversion and paramilitary operations. The CIA, which had been primarily an information-gathering body for the State Department, was transformed into the primary instrument for subversion and sabotage. . . .

Nowhere has the CIA been given a bolder opportunity, or more clearly revealed the weaknesses of Cold War policy, than in Vietnam. From around 1954 to 1964 the Agency was the power behind the South Vietnamese government, army, and police force. It also organized an undercover army and air force to fight a secret war in Laos.

Globalism Outdated

Globalism is no longer a viable policy. American bases are unpleasant symbols in the Third World and revive imperial memories. In turn, Soviet troops in Afghanistan have only served to discredit Soviet policy elsewhere in the world. The days when one nation can write the history of another—especially when that country is determined to write its own—are over. We learned that in Vietnam; the Soviets may learn it in Afghanistan. It is a painful and costly lesson. We need not forget it now.

Robert J. Bresler, *USA Today*, May 1980.

Why did the United States and the CIA commit so much of their time and money to Vietnam and Southeast Asia? The United States first supported the French financially in their attempt to recolonize Vietnam. Ho Chi Minh fought and won his war of independence against France. The United States would not support Ho Chi Minh because he was a socialist, and he was forced to accept aid from the Communist bloc.

A peace agreement was finally worked out at Geneva in 1954 by many interested nations, which provided for Vietnam's temporary division into North and South. Elections were scheduled for 1956, and whoever won them was to govern a united Vietnam. Meanwhile Ho Chi Minh ruled North Vietnam. John Foster Dulles, secretary of state under President Eisenhower, refused to accept the agreement. Dulles feared that any free election would result in a landslide for the socialist Ho Chi Minh.

John Foster Dulles and his brother Alan Dulles now began to utilize the CIA in an effort to forestall the holding of elections and the possibility of South Vietnam becoming a Communist state. To achieve this, the U.S. and the CIA policy makers selected Ngo Dinh Diem and set him up as premier of South Vietnam. CIA agents ran the public relations campaign that put Diem into office. They gained control of the South Vietnamese army, bureaucracy, and police for him. They also taught him how to rig elections so that he always won by a large majority in South Vietnam. The United States paid the major cost of the running of Diem's government, and almost the entire cost of the maintenance of his military forces, the ARVN.

Failure of Goals

With all this help, the United States hoped that Diem would become popular enough to woo the people away from Ho Chi Minh. Instead, Diem turned into a corrupt and ruthless dictator who put his family into office, grew rich from the narcotics trade, and terrorized the Vietnamese. While he expropriated the peasants' land and gave it to his rich friends, his secret police executed thousands of peasants as "Communist sympathizers."

In reaction, the peasants formed a rebel organization, the National Liberation Front, together with a loosely organized guerrilla army known as the Vietcong. Its jungle warfare against Diem's army was successful from the start, both because the Vietcong fought with conviction and because they had increasing support from the mass of South Vietnamese peasants. The ARVN, Diem's forces, were no match for the Vietcong. Most of them had no stomach for fighting their countrymen, whose goals were the reunification of North and South and American withdrawal from Vietnam. . . .

The efforts made by the CIA to implement Cold War policies in Vietnam were obviously counterproductive and unsuccessful. There are indications that despite a current Congressional attempt to curtail their activities, efforts are being made to utilize them or similar agencies to carry on in much the same manner as before. Now that the veil of secrecy that surrounds the CIA has to some extent been lifted, U.S. citizens should determine whether or not they want similar activities to continue. . . .

The Difficulty of Dissent

Thoughtful citizens who would like to debate, discuss, or dissent from a mindless support of the Cold War have often found it inadvisable to do so, particularly after the persecutions of the McCarthy Era. Ordinary Americans who do so are smeared as unpatriotic, and dedicated government and military officials who do so risk their careers.

In this climate, it is easy to understand why it was possible for the Cold War to continue in Vietnam for almost eighteen years and for Lyndon Johnson and Richard Nixon to fight an unpopular "hot" war there for another ten years. But even then they might not have been able to carry it off without using tactics to suppress dissent among U.S. citizens similar to the Cold War tactics used against people in foreign nations.

Cold War Rhetoric

In order to "sell" its Cold War program to the American people, so that the Presidency would have a free hand in exercising cold and hot war policies, the government engages in an enormous program of "public relations and information," consisting of a barrage of speeches, statements, and press handouts, amounting to the almost continual indoctrination of the American people concerning the evils of Communism. This Cold War rhetoric has varied only slightly down through the years. Its intensity is determined by the need to gain citizen support for political purposes, wars, military appropriations, and to enable the President to have a free hand in foreign policy. After more than a half century of such intermittent incantations and indoctrination, few citizens seem to have questioned the unsupported accusations and the half truths that make cold Warism an important part of the psyche of the American people. . . .

There is nothing affirmative about a disaster except the lessons learned that can prevent a similar happening. We now know what happens when the final discretion in matters of war and peace is left solely in the hands of political leaders. There has never been a better time for U.S. citizens to examine the facts and to exercise their democratic right to be heard. American citizens in this democracy will thus have the power to participate in the most important decision of our time: *How can we best save the United States from future wars that could lead to nuclear disaster?*

"Communism is a great threat to our well-being and security. . . . We must look to protect the interest of this nation at home and abroad."

The US Must Maintain Cold War Principles

Jeremiah A. Denton Jr.

Formerly a Rear Admiral in the US Navy, Jeremiah A. Denton Jr. is a US Senator from Alabama. He served in Vietnam and was a prisoner of war there. In the following viewpoint he discusses the wrong lessons he believes the nation is taking from the Vietnam defeat. He also explains why he believes it is essential that the US maintain its policy of containing communism.

As you read, consider the following questions:

1. What are the "wrong lessons" of Vietnam, according to Senator Denton?
2. What does he say are the "right lessons"?
3. What are the "three truths" Senator Denton believes must be emphasized by the media and the educational system?

Jeremiah A. Denton Jr., "Putting Vietnam into Perspective," *The American Legion*, March 1980. Copyright 1980, The American Legion Magazine; reprinted by permission.

After a career in the United States Navy and considerable formal and informal education in international affairs, I am painfully conscious that our nation is floundering in confusion which accelerated in the late 1960s. I was then a prisoner of war in Communist North Vietnam.

I was directly affected and know firsthand what went on over there. That's why I feel I can say, "Let's look at it squarely . . . We lost the Vietnam War." In the process, we also lost some other definable and undefinable things, though perhaps only temporarily.

Wrong Lessons

To help insure the loss is indeed temporary, we cannot remain numbly silent while others who would wreck America draw wrong lessons from the experience and etch them indelibly into the conscience of our nation. Some of the wrong lessons are:

• The war was an immoral war in which the United States slaughtered innocent civilians;

• Those who burned their draft cards were right; the cause in Vietnam was wrong;

• Military service is not the "in" thing and is for volunteers only;

• The United States can no longer afford to take a major role in influencing world affairs.

I would not say the military as a group is innocent of *all* errors in Vietnam. Nor could that be said of *any* military in any other war in history. But in no other war did any nation lean farther over backward trying to avoid killing innocents than did we—in spite of exceptions such as My Lai.

I believe that of all the wars fought in our history, our armed forces should rightly be most proud of their service and sacrifice in Vietnam. Our services "did their thing" under conditions that tested *esprit* in terms of loyalty and courage—tested them as no previous war ever did.

We endured the test and our military honor remains untarnished. Discipline shown in campaigns was outshown only by the discipline displayed after the war when the issue which had been decided militarily at such cost was being obfuscated in subsequent non-military actions.

Right Cause

But the cause in Vietnam was not wrong.

The issue—the cause there at stake—was whether the relative degree of freedom enjoyed in those countries (one of which was an ally to whose defense we were committed by treaty and the word of four Presidents) was worth preserving against an *externally* designed and empowered aggression to bring them into an utter vacuum of freedom.

The present-day holocaust in Cambodia and the late, but real, blood baths in South Vietnam and Laos have proved that our basic commitment was justified. Perhaps one-third of Cambodia's population has been slain since the war ended. Communist jackals are now fighting over the carcass of Southeast Asia. Tens of millions of human beings were doomed by our needless cop-out when Congress cut off bombing in Cambodia—bombing which was helping those trying to resist the Khmer Rouge.

The final straw came when we withdrew material aid just when South Vietnam had finally achieved the solidarity to defend itself effectively if equipment were forthcoming. When we withdrew our support, both Cambodia and South Vietnam were doomed. They fell as I knew they must.

Jeremiah A. Denton Jr.

We did make errors in Vietnam, and it is easy for me to understand how many well-meaning Americans became unsupportive of the war then. And, even now, they still suffer from what I call the "Vietnam Hangover."

Among government officials and civilians, the Vietnam Hangover has been manifested by doing away with the draft; creating a national mood making possible the invasion of Angola by Cuban troops carried by Russian ships; making possible the enslavement not only of South Vietnam, but also of Cambodia and Laos; making possible the endangering of the achievement of a proper structure for a much-needed Salt II Agreement. Afghanistan is, politically, a fallen domino. Zaire and the Horn of Africa are in peril. The energy shortage and the fantastic deficit in balance of payments are not unrelated to the Vietnam Hangover. The situation in Iran is shocking, but is only a continuation of the more rapidly-falling dominoes. *We cannot afford to continue to act from a false perspective.*

Our initial error, which tended to create conditions which led to other errors, was that we began in Vietnam with a too-gradualistic military approach. A small portion of the blame for that error belongs with some in the military. But most military opinion, even early on, was to apply what the U.S. Army calls "shock."

We did not apply "shock." We continued the gradualistic buildup. Personally, I believe it would have been difficult given the political factor, if not impossible, to apply that shock by U.S. *land* forces in South Vietnam. MacArthur and Ridgeway tried to pass on that bitterly learned legacy.

In my opinion, based on personal contact with the Vietnamese Communists for nearly eight years, that shock *could* have been applied easily, cheaply and humanely by air and naval means in 1965 or any subsequent year. It was finally and effectively applied in 1972 with the strategic bombing of military targets around Hanoi and by mining of and bombing near Haiphong, their major port. If 10 percent of that air and naval shock had been applied in the north in 1965, the war would have been over in a week, no freedom would have been lost and we would still have a correct perspective.

Orgy of Confusion

Our great folly was not in calling a series of losing plays, for some plays were bound to be ill-conceived in that difficult game. Our great folly was that after calling and executing a winning series, we snatched defeat from the mouth of victory in an orgy of confusion. Most Americans still have no idea that the strategic bombing applied in December 1972 was a complete American victory. The issue was amazingly dropped in national confusion following the war.

The confusion arose during the war from an over-emphasis on

132

two valid ideals and an under-emphasis on two valid facts. *The two valid ideals are these:* (1) War is a prospect to be avoided if at all possible without the sacrifice of important national interests; (2) Violence against human beings is abhorrent to the concept of civilization.

The two valid facts which were under-emphasized are these: (1) Notwithstanding the stated noble aim of the United Nations to outlaw aggression, Communism is a force which has found effective means of conducting aggression. These means constitute externally-supported subversions to overthrow imperfect governments, and conquest by proxy nations conducting ambiguous forms of aggression. In selective instances like Vietnam and Korea, the United States has justly chosen to commit military force to stop Communist aggression after diplomatic means were exhausted.

Communist Threat

Communism is a great threat to our well-being and security; it is the antithesis of our principles regarding religion, family, free enterprise and the government-citizen relationship. We need to continue to pursue international ideals but, until ideas become reality, we must look to protect the interests of this nation at home and abroad. We need to continue to help relatively free nations to survive against Communism and help them with ideas and material support.

Jeremiah A. Denton Jr.

War is a last resort because war is hell, but slavery is an even worse hell, kills more people, lasts longer, and—if Communist aggression, which is really the imposition of slavery, is condoned by mankind today—civilization will be set back 500 years, thereby returning the conduct of international affairs to the rules of the jungle.

Deterrence of Communism

I am not saying that war is necessarily the only way to check Communism—deterrence is the best way. I am saying that the *willingness* to use *decisive* force when justified, and the perceived possession of that force constitute the only deterrence or actual combat combination they understand. It is the only combination that can keep the peace, prevent further aggressive spread of Communism, and protect our essential national interests abroad. Communism has some differences in form around the world, but it is still basically the enslavement of people.

(2) The second fact is that when military force is committed in a war, the object is not to twist gradually the enemy's arm, but

quickly to break his will. This axiom is especially true when dealing with as small an antagonist as North Vietnam. I quite agree,
however, that losing 50,000 Americans is not properly called police
action—it is war, requiring national backing and congressional
commitment.

As to the anti-war ideals, I agree with them. Mankind took a
while to address these ideals. Civilization itself took mankind
millions of years to achieve. Civilization is only about 5,000
years old, is fragile and has failed at times in a given society. But
civilization has advanced in efforts to eliminate war as a routine
means of settling international differences, as well as in efforts to
alleviate some of the unnecessary brutalities of war. Particularly, the late 19th and the first half of the 20th centuries saw
important steps in this direction with the Hague Tribunal,
Geneva Conventions, the League of Nations and the United
Nations. Perhaps we can dismiss the present UN as a major factor, but we cannot ignore the fact that the League and the UN did
prevent many wars which would otherwise have occurred, and
they limited the time and scope of some that did.

During and after World War II, the United States became a
major leader in this trend. Korea was a UN action. Our going to
the defense of Vietnam was in accordance with the UN Charter.
Both actions were not only *not immoral*, but were also idealistic.
The United States had not much selfish interest in Korea or
South Vietnam, but as a major nation interested in the continuing development of inhibition against aggression by truly immoral nations, we committed first our diplomatic efforts, then
our treasure and then our blood.

Those are the two facts and the two ideals.

On another front we must consider the NATO alliance—an
anti-aggressive, truly defensive alliance which has worked.
Since 1949, NATO-alliance nations have done some fighting,
but, per-capita-per-year, they have lost a fraction of the lives lost
throughout the rest of their history. NATO brought Soviet Communist expansion in Europe to a halt without a single casualty.
But the Communist resort to ambiguous proxy aggression and
their conquests by subversion are the tactics for which we have
not yet found an effective answer.

To me, the big picture is that our nation became confused on
these points, among others. We lost the issue as well as more than
50,000 Americans. And we lost some important degree of credibility in the world.

Our nation and others have survived even worse confusion such
as our own Civil War. But the consequences of the loss of credibility still continue and they hamper our conduct of international affairs. . . .

Our nation urgently needs a return to an informal bipartisan approach to foreign policy which we enjoyed from about 1942-1965. To achieve that approach, we need to help our citizenry attain a better national understanding of our place in world affairs. . . .

Our citizens are confused on vital issues.

Essential Truths

Our nation's people need to be told the truth. An informed citizenry is essential to survival of a democracy. The three truths which need to be emphasized now by the media and our educational systems are these:

• With its imperfections, the United States of America is the best, in terms of its record of national and international justice, of any major nation in the world's history.

Abandoning American Values

An acceptance of the simplistic slogan "No more Vietnams" not only may encourage international disorder, but could mean abandoning basic American values. As John Stuart Mill pointed out more than 100 years ago, "The doctrine of non-intervention, to be a legitimate principle of morality, must be accepted by all governments. The despots must consent to be bound by it as well as the free States. Unless they do, the profession of it by freeing countries comes but to this miserable issue, that the wrong side may help the wrong, but the right must not help the right." . . .

America cannot and should not be the world's policeman, but, it can be argued, the U.S. has a moral obligation to support nations in their endeavor to remain independent when we, and we alone, possess the means to do so."

Guenter Lewy, *America in Vietnam*, 1978.

• Communism is a great threat to our well-being and security; it is the antithesis of our principles regarding religion, family, free enterprise and the government-citizen relationship. We need to continue to pursue international ideals but, until ideals become reality, we must look to protect the interests of this nation at home and abroad. We need to continue to help relatively free nations to survive against Communism and help them with ideas and material support.

• We must be true to our own valid national principles which, most importantly, brought us to this pinnacle of material and spiritual greatness. We cannot continue a trend of blindly individualistic selfishness, and promote the so-called new morality which is really just the old immorality. We must try again to progress toward becoming one nation under God. No matter how far we have slipped personally or nationally, we can attain well-being and security again if we act again as if we are "relying on Divine Providence."

Until we regain among our citzenry an understanding and necessary emphasis on acting from those three truths, we shall continue on the drunken road to disaster.

It's time to act! Let's clean up our minds, clean up our acts and get the great American show back on the road.

"We as a whole people participated in the evil of the Johnson administration."

US Involvement Was Evil

M. Scott Peck

M. Scott Peck, a practicing psychiatrist, is recognized as a leader in the current movement toward the integration of psychology and spirituality. Educated at Harvard and Case Western Reserve, he served in the Army Medical Corps during the Vietnam war years of 1963 to 1972. The following viewpoint, excerpted from Dr. Peck's book, *People of the Lie: The Hope for Healing Human Evil*, states that America was the villain in Vietnam and its policies were evil. Basing his conclusions on his study of evil in the field of psychiatry and his experiences in the Army, Dr. Peck claims America is likely to repeat the mistake unless it recognizes and eradicates the twin causes of evil—laziness and narcissism.

As you read, consider the following questions:

1. Why does the author think America's Vietnam involvement was based on an unrealistic idea?
2. What does the author mean when he claims the real reasons for America's involvement in Vietnam were laziness and narcissism?
3. Do you agree with the author's claim that American citizens were ultimately responsible for American evil in Vietnam?

Basically, we fought the war because of a combination of three attitudes: (1) communism was a monolithic evil force hostile to human freedom in general and American freedom in particular; (2) it was America's duty as the world's most economically powerful nation to lead the opposition against communism; and (3) communism should be opposed wherever it arose by whatever means necessary.

This combination of attitudes comprising the American posture in international relations had its origins in the late 1940s and early 1950s. Immediately following the end of World War II, the Communist USSR, with extraordinary speed and aggressiveness, imposed its political domination over almost the entirety of eastern Europe: Finland, Poland, Lithuania, Latvia, Estonia, East Germany, Czechoslovakia, Hungary, Bulgaria, Albania, and presumably Yugoslavia. Seemingly only by American money and American arms and leadership was the rest of Europe prevented from falling into the clutches of communism. Then just as we were bolstering the defense against communism's western flank, it exploded in the East, with the whole of China falling under Communist domination in 1950 almost overnight. And already the forces of communism were clearly threatening to expand through Vietnam and Malaya. The line had to be drawn. Given the explosive expansion of communism on all sides of the USSR, it is no wonder that we perceived it in 1954 as an evil monolithic force, so dangerously threatening to the entire world that we needed to become engaged against it in a life-and-death struggle that left little room for moral scruples.

Communism Not Monolithic Nor Evil

The problem, however, is that by a scant dozen years later there was a wealth of evidence to indicate that communism was not (if, in fact, it had ever been) a force that was either monolithic or necessarily evil. Yugoslavia was clearly independent of the USSR, and Albania was becoming so. China and the USSR were no longer allies but potential enemies. As for Vietnam, any slightly discerning examination of its history revealed it to be a traditional enemy of China. The impelling force behind the Vietnamese Communists at that point in their history was not the expansion of communism but nationalism and resistance to colonial domination. Moreover, it had also become clear that despite the constraints on their civil liberties, the people in Communist societies were generally faring better than they had under their pre-Communist forms of government. It was also clear that the people in many non-Communist societies, with whose governments we had allied ourselves, were suffering violations of human rights that matched those of the USSR and China.

Our military involvement in Vietnam began in the period be-

SANDERS IN THE MILWAUKEE JOURNAL

*"What shall I put
down as the reason for dying?"*

tween 1954 and 1956, when the idea of a monolithic Communist menace seemed realistic. A dozen years later it was no longer realistic. Yet at precisely the time when it had ceased to be realistic, when we should have been readjusting our strategy and withdrawing from Vietnam, we began to seriously escalate our military involvement there in defense of obsolescent attitudes. Why? Why, beginning around 1964, did America's behavior in Vietnam become increasingly unrealistic and inappropriate? There are two reasons: laziness and—once again—narcissism.

Attitudes have a kind of inertia. Once set in motion, they will keep going, even in the face of the evidence. To change an attitude requires a considerable amount of work and suffering. The process must begin either in an effortfully maintained posture of constant self-doubt and criticism or else in a painful acknowledgement that what we thought was right all along may not be right after all. Then it proceeds into a state of confusion. This state is quite uncomfortable; we no longer seem to know what is right or wrong or which way to go. But it is a state of openness and therefore of learning and growing. It is only from the quicksand of confusion that we are able to leap to the new and better vision.

Lazy and Self-Satisfied Leaders

I think we may properly regard the men who governed America at the time of MyLai—the Johnson administration—as lazy and self-satisfied. They, like most more ordinary individuals, had little taste for intellectual confusion—nor for the effort involved in maintaining a "posture of constant self-doubt and criticism." They assumed that the attitudes they had developed toward the "monolithic Communist menace" during the preceding two decades were still the right attitudes. Although the evidence was obviously mounting to throw their attitudes into question, they ignored it. To do otherwise would have placed them in the painful and difficult position of having to rethink their attitudes. They did not take up the work required. It was easier to proceed blindly, as if nothing had changed.

Thus far we have been focusing on the laziness involved in "clinging to old maps" and attitudes that have become obsolete. Let us also examine the narcissism. We are our attitudes. If someone criticizes an attitude of mine, I feel he or she is criticizing *me*. If one of my opinions is proved wrong, then *I* have been wrong. My self-image of perfection has been shattered. Individuals and nations cling to obsolete and outworn ideas not simply because it requires work to change them but also because, in their narcissism, they cannot imagine that their ideas and views could be wrong. They believe themselves to be right. Oh, we are quick to superficially disclaim our infallibility, but deep inside most of us, particularly when we have apparently been successful and powerful, we consider ourselves invariably in the right. It was this kind of narcissism, manifested in our behavior in Vietnam, that Senator William Fulbright referred to as "the arrogance of power."

Evil Policy

Ordinarily, if our noses are rubbed in the evidence, we can tolerate the painful narcissistic injury involved, admit our need for change, and correct our outlook. But as is the case with certain individuals, the narcissism of whole nations may at times exceed the normal bounds. When this happens, the nation—instead of readjusting in light of the evidence—sets about attempting to destroy the evidence. This was what America was up to in the 1960s. The situation in Vietnam presented us with evidence of the fallibility of our world view and the limits of our potency. So, rather than rethinking it, we set about to destroy the situation in Vietnam, and all of Vietnam with it if necessary.

Which was evil. Evil has already been defined most simply as the use of political power to destroy others for the purpose of defending or preserving the integrity of one's sick self. Since it had become outmoded, our monolithic view of communism was part of our national sick self—no longer adaptive and realistic. In the failure of the Diem regime, which we sponsored, in the failure of all our "advisers" and Green Berets and massive economic and military aid to counteract the expansion of the Viet Cong, the sickness or wrongness of our policies was exposed to ourselves. Rather than alter these policies, however, we launched a full-scale war to preserve them intact. Rather than admit what would have been a minor failure in 1964, we set about rapidly escalating the war to prove ourselves right at the expense of the Vietnamese people and their self-aspirations. The issue ceased to be what was right for Vietnam and became an issue of our infallibility and preserving our national "honor."

Squalid National Effort

Our waging of the war, not our losing of it, disgraced us in men's eyes. . . .

Our national effort was squalid in concept and execution. We tried to bend an ancient and civilized people to our will, and we failed, but not before we used our overwhelming power and technology to the full. We cratered vast stretches of Vietnam with our bombs. We destroyed villages without number and herded their inhabitants into stockades. We poisoned the wells, the forests and the farms with Agent Orange. We bulldozed millions of acres of forest and jungle.

All in all we killed over two million of them, mostly civilians. We napalmed women and children. Many of our soldiers disintegrated and did terrible things which haunt them today.

Charles Owen Rice, *The Catholic Bulletin,* January 13, 1982.

Strangely enough, on a certain level, President Johnson and the men of his administration knew that what they were doing was evil. Otherwise, why all the lying? It was so bizarre and seemingly out of character that it is difficult for us merely to recall the extraordinary national dishonesty of those days, a scant fifteen years ago. Even the excuse President Johnson gave in order to begin bombing North Vietnam and escalate the war in 1964—the "Gulf of Tonkin Incident"—was apparently a deliberate fraud. Through this fraud he obtained from Congress the authority to wage the war without Congress ever formally declaring it (which was its constitutional responsibility). Then he set about "borrowing" the money to pay for the war—diverting funds earmarked for other programs and extorting "savings bonds" from the salaries of federal employees—so that the American public would not have to immediately pay increased taxes or feel the burden of the escalation.

This book is entitled *People of the Lie* because lying is both a cause and a manifestation of evil. It is partly by their lying that we recognize the evil. President Johnson clearly did not want the American people to fully know and understand what he was doing in Vietnam in their name. He knew that what he was doing would be ultimately unacceptable to them. His defrauding the electorate was not only evil in itself but was also evidence of his awareness of the evil of his actions, since he felt compelled to cover them up.

Responsibility of All Americans

But it would be a mistake and a potentially evil rationalization itself for us to blame the evil of those days entirely on the Johnson administration. We must ask why Johnson was successful in defrauding us. Why did we allow ourselves to be defrauded for so long? Not everyone was. A very small minority was quick to recognize that the wool was being pulled over our eyes, that "something rather dark and bloody" was being perpetrated by the nation. But why were most of us not aroused to ire or suspicion or even significant concern about the nature of the war?

Once again we are confronted with our all-too-human laziness and narcissism. Basically, it was just too much trouble. We all had our lives to lead—doing our day-to-day jobs, buying new cars, painting our houses, sending our kids to college. As the majority of members of any group are content to let the leadership be exercised by the few, so as a citizenry we were content to let the government "do its thing." It was Johnson's job to lead, ours to follow. The citizenry was simply too lethargic to become aroused. Besides, we shared with Johnson his enormous large-as-Texas narcissism. . . .

By allowing ourselves to be easily and blatantly defrauded, we as a whole people participated in the evil of the Johnson adminstration. The evil—the years of lying and manipulation—of the Johnson administration was directly conducive to the whole atmosphere of lying and manipulation and evil that pervaded our presence in Vietnam during those years. . . .

Americans as the Villains

I am convinced it will be the judgment of history—that America was the aggressor in that war during those years. Ours were the choices that were most morally reprehensible. We were the villains.

But how could we—we Americans—be villains? The Germans and the Japanese in 1941, certainly. The Russians, yes. But the Americans? Surely we are not a villainous people. If we were villains, we must have been unwitting ones. This I concede; we were largely unwitting. But how does it come about that a person or a group or an entire nation is an unwitting villain?. . .

The term "unwitting villain" is particularly appropriate because our villainy lay in our unwittingness. We became villains precisely because we did not have our wits about us. The word "wit" in this regard refers to knowledge. We were villains out of ignorance. Just as what went on at MyLai was covered up for a year primarily because the troops of Task Force Barker did not know they had done something radically wrong, so America waged the war because it did not know that what it was doing was villainous.

Threat to World

The lesson of Vietnam was that the United States, not the Soviet Union and certainly not Communism, represented the greatest threat to the security and well-being of the peoples of the world.

Norman Podhoretz, *Why We Were in Vietnam*, 1983.

I used to ask the troops on their way to battle in Vietnam what they knew about the war and its relationship to Vietnamese history. The enlisted men knew nothing. Ninety percent of the junior officers knew nothing. What little the senior officers and few junior officers did know was generally solely what they had been taught in the highly biased programs of their military schools. It was astounding. At least 95 percent of the men going off to risk their very lives did not even have the slightest knowledge of what the war was about. I also talked to Department of Defense civilians who directed the war and discovered a similar atrocious ignorance of Vietnamese history. The fact of the matter is that as a nation we did not even know why we were waging the war.

How could this have been? How could a whole people have gone to war not knowing why? The answer is simple. As a people we were too lazy to learn and too arrogant to think we needed to learn. We felt that whatever way we happened to perceive things was the right way without any further study. And that whatever we did was the right thing to do without reflection. We were so wrong because we never seriously considered that we might not be right. With our laziness and narcissism feeding each other, we marched off to impose our will on the Vietnamese people by bloodshed with practically no idea of what was involved. Only when we—the mightiest nation on earth—consistently suffered defeat at the hands of the Vietnamese did we in significant numbers begin to take the trouble to learn what we had done.

So it is that our "Christian" nation became a nation of villains. So it has been with other nations in the past, and so it will be with other nations—including our own once again—in the future. As a nation and as a race, we shall not be immune to war until such a time as we have made much further progress toward eradicating from our human nature the twin progenitors of evil: laziness and narcissism.

"Perhaps the only way to judge the 'morality' of the Vietnam war...is to examine who the enemy was....The bloody record of the last seven years answers all these questions."

US Involvement Was Just

Jim Guirard

Jim Guirard is a government affairs consultant, freelance writer, and lecturer in Washington, DC. In the following viewpoint he discusses the morality of the Vietnam war in terms of the enemy. He says that the US was confused about the nature of the enemy, but that by viewing what has happened in Vietnam since the US left, one can easily see the moral necessity of trying to prevent that evil.

As you read, consider the following questions:

1. How does the author say we should evaluate the nature of the enemy we fought in Vietnam?
2. What concensus does Mr. Guirard believe the US should have come to?
3. Why, according to the author, should even anti-war activists be able to accept the morality of US involvement in Vietnam?

Jim Guirard, "Vietnam: The War and the Memorial," *The Washington Times*, November 8, 1982. CC The Washington Times, 1982; reprinted with permission.

The continuing controversy over the design (the resulting symbolism) of the Vietnam Veterans Memorial keeps lively the perennial debate as to whether we should have fought that war.

In terms of the suitability of the monument, the relevant question is not whether Vietnam was *wise* or *winnable* but whether it was fundamentally a "just" war. Was the cause for which we fought a "moral" one? Were those now being memorialized the good guys or the bad guys in that conflict?

Memorial Design Controversy

Proponents of the present design tend to be those who were (and remain) of the antiwar sentiment—both as to Vietnam in particular and as to armed conflict in general. They favor the below-ground black walls on which the names of the war dead are inscribed in the order in which they died.

Many of these people are fighting a proposal to add a large American flag and a modest statue of three soldiers to the memorial—even though the statue is not in the "heroic" form typical of most war memorials. If the statue and the flag are installed, they want them not at the center of the memorial but far off to one side, preferably out of sight.

Opponents of the monument's design are, generally speaking, those who felt (and continue to feel) that our effort in Vietnam was in defense of a just and moral cause—a cause which should have been pursued to victory.

Many of these people argue that the monument's subterranean design reflects negatively on the cause for which the Vietnam War was fought. They feel that many truly heroic veterans are being damned by faint and inappropriate praise. Better, some argue, to have no monument at all than one which seems to apologize for, rather than to honor, those memorialized. Placement of the flag at the apex of the monument and the statue in some other prominent position nearby would be a partial concession to that point of view.

And between these two groups are those, probably a majority, who care less about the particular design than about the fact that a long-overdue memorial has finally been installed in a place of prominence in the nation's capitol. They simply want the pain, the confusion and the legacy of national discord to go away and be forgotten. Ambivalent about the war itself, they care little about whatever subtle meanings might be hidden in the design of its memorial.

How do we judge which sentiment is right? Perhaps the only way to judge the "morality" of the Vietnam War (and, thus, the suitability of the memorial to its veterans) is to examine *who the enemy was*. What was the true identity of those we went there to oppose?

- Were they the "liberators" they claimed to be, or were they themselves the oppressors and imperialists from whom they pretended to offer liberation?

• Did they intend to institute "social justice" and "popular reform," or did they always intend to impose a grisly dictatorship?

• Did they really offer "democratic" socialism, or is their brand of socialism any less despotic and genocidal than Adolf Hitler's or Idi Amin's?

• Were they at heart the "progressives" and anti-fascists they seemed to many naive Americans and Europeans to be, or were they in truth a most vicious and uncompromising *variety* of fascists?

The bloody record of the last several years answers all these questions with great certainty. The promises of the "liberators" were patently false. The warnings of those who predicted repression and brutality for South Vietnam at the hands of the communists were entirely well-founded.

Barbaric Communism

Even such deeply committed antiwar activists as entertainer Joan Baez and liberal-intellectual author Susan Sontag have seen the terrible truth. And even more impressive, they have had the courage and intellectual honesty—*unlike many of their peers*—to admit their previous mistaken impressions about the true nature of communism. Miss Baez went so far as to sponsor full-page newspaper ads condemning the barbaric repression of human rights which chased hundreds of thousands of "boat people" from Vietnam.

Noble Cause

It is time we recognized that ours was, in truth, a noble cause. A small country newly free from colonial rule sought our help in establishing self-rule and the means of self-defense against a totalitarian neighbor bent on conquest. We dishonor the memory of 50,000 young Americans who died in that cause when we give way to feelings of guilt as if we were doing something shameful, and we have been shabby in our treatment of those who returned. They fought as well and as bravely as any Americans have ever fought in any war. They deserve our gratitude, our respect and our continuing concern.

Ronald Reagan, speech, 1980.

More recently Miss Sontag examined both the genocidal horrors of Southeast Asia and the Gestapo-like military dictatorship in Poland and came to the following conclusion:

"Not only is fascism (and overt military rule) the probable destiny of all communist societies—especially when their populations are moved to revolt—but communism is in itself a variant, the most successful variant, of fascism. Fascism with a human face.

147

If, as Susan Sontag implies, we were in Vietnam fighting *fascists*, which is precisely what the Vietnamese communists have proven themselves to be, were we not completely justified in opposing their tyranny? Is not anti-fascism by definition a "moral" cause for any true civil-libertarian?

Anyone who doubts Miss Sontag's neo-liberal conclusion as to the inherently fascist character of the ultra-left should try composing a detailed essay on human rights, arguing the particular theme: "The typical communist regime is *not* fascist." It cannot possibly be done. Upon the promotion and protection of what list of human rights could the proponent of such a thesis possibly base his argument?

No less an expert on the essence of fascism than Adolf Hitler conceded the essential kinship between his brand of "national socialism" (Naziism) and the communist variety: "The petit bourgeois Social Democrat and the trade union boss," he said, "will never make a National Socialist, but the communist always will."

Tragic Lack of Consensus

The tragedy of the Vietnam era was that America was never able to develop a consensus as to who the enemy was—good guy or bad guy. Incredibly, we still cannot. Not even in the wake of the "boat people." Not even in the face of the "yellow rain" atrocities on Cambodian and Laotian tribesmen. Not even as 500,000 political prisoners are herded off to Siberia as "guest workers."

The continued anti-Vietnam War bias of many honest and caring people is traceable to the simple fact that they have not rethought the issue in light of these horrendous crimes. Eventually, they will see the light and will respond appropriately—except, of course, for those few whose pacifism and isolationism is so absolute that they would not approve of armed resistance even to the likes of Hitler, or Pol Pot or Idi Amin. Still others, who might best be called pseudo-liberals, do indeed know the grisly facts but have chosen both personally and publicly to ignore and to deny their true meaning.

At the personal level, they appear to be slaves to an ego factor which persuades many (particularly the liberal-intellectuals) that they are far too well educated and too clever to have been so thoroughly duped by anyone—and surely not by a bunch of fascists masking as fellow liberals and progressives.

At the political and professional levels the psuedo-liberals must guard against "revisionist" conclusions about Vietnam which might overturn many an applecart. At risk are the vested interests of many well-funded social and political movements, the positions of prominent office-holders, the reputations of distinguished scholars and journalists, and even the power balance between political parties. All of these might be substantially undermined by a wide-spread awakening to the notion that staunch anti-communism is, after all, a noble cause for true liberals.

Back to the monument. Now that it has been dedicated, it is too late to discard its non-heroic, sunken design. The best that can be expected for the moment is that it will be modified by placing the flag and the statue prominently at the center of the monument rather than somewhere at the periphery.

Then, as the neo-liberal view of communism gradually takes hold among true progressives they will help form a new consensus. They will join the more traditional anti-communists in having the monument modified further—to acknowledge more adequately both the heroism of those who served in Vietnam and the inherent justice and morality of the cause for which the war was fought.

Eventually, too, a consensus should evolve that Vietnam was a *winnable* cause as well—if only we had not dragged ourselves down to defeat in a vicious family feud over who the enemy was and why, in the name of human rights, he should have been defeated.

The Ability to Empathize

The ability to emphathize, to see life and experience its joys and problems through another person's eyes and feelings, is a helpful skill to acquire if one is to learn from the life situations of others.

Consider the following situation taken from the book *Nam* by Mark Baker.

We got into this village and herded all the people together, maybe sixty–seventy people. Women, children, everybody. We burned all their homes to the ground. We thought they were being evacuated.

At the last second I broke squelch. You don't talk on the radio because the enemy can triangulate, they can hear you. You just do not talk on the radio. I broke squelch, because I thought they would move these people out, relocate them to a POW camp. Question them, find out who's doing what and release the rest of them.

A guy gets on the radio and says, "Waste 'em."

I wasn't going to talk on the radio. I broke squelch again—twice. The guy goes, "Waste 'em."

I said, "Waste what?"

"Waste everybody that you've got."

"You're talking about sixty–seventy people, some of whom may be friendlies. Are you aware of that?"

He said, "Waste 'em."

"Can I have your name and rank?" I said, because I was not going to kill all those people.

"Sonny boy," he said, "I assure you that I outrank you by five ranks and twenty years. And I'm telling you to waste 'em."

"How do I know you're not a civilian?" I said. "You may be a field agent for the CIA or something. I'm not going to 'waste 'em' until I get somebody on this. . .radio who will tell me who the hell they are and by what authority I'm doing the wasting. At that particular point, I might do something about it."

Two people who claimed to be very, *very* high-ranking officials got on the radio. One of them said to me, "By order of the Commander in Chief of the United States Armed Forces, I'm telling you that the previous transmission given you is what you are to adhere to."

Excerpt from pp. 176-177 "We got into this village. . .The women, the men, the children, everyone." In NAM by Mark Baker. Copyright © 1981 by Mark Baker. By permission of William Morrow & Company.

"I really can't believe what you're telling me."

"We really don't care if you believe. Waste 'em."

So I got with eight of my men. The other two were guarding the villagers. I told them we'd just had an order on the radio to emulsify these people. What should we do? We had to talk for an hour.

It was a double bind. If we did it, we would be very ill at ease with ourselves. If we didn't do it, we'd be in a lot of trouble when we got back. There was no right answer.

But I had a couple of people who really enjoyed killing quite a bit. They were the ones on guard. I told them what the situation was. They couldn't wait. They grinned from ear to ear. They pulled back, made all the villagers lie down on the ground with their hands behind their backs. Then these guys wasted them. The women, the men, the children, everyone.

Instructions:

Try to imagine how the following individuals would react in this situation. What reasons might they give for their actions. Try to imagine and explain their feelings.

The patrol leader

The two soldiers who did the actual killing

The two high-ranking officials on the radio that ordered the killings

The victims

A 19-year-old soldier on his first patrol in Vietnam

A 36-year-old career soldier with two years to go before retirement who is a member of the patrol

The commander-in-chief, President Johnson

William Mahedy, the author of viewpoint one in chapter three

Peter Marin, the author of viewpoint two in chapter three

You

"Blind national will, false national pride and an unending belief in U.S. military power...led us into war and again could slip us into a senseless conflict."

The US Should Not Act from Arrogance

Thomas C. Fox

Thomas C. Fox is editor of the *National Catholic Reporter*. In the following viewpoint he discusses what he views as three major flaws in US perception of world problems and how to deal with them. Rather than "revise" the ideas about US involvement in Vietnam to make the US look morally correct, he states that the nation must squarely face these flaws and revise the way it deals with other countries.

As you read, consider the following questions:

1. What are the three lessons Mr. Fox sees in Vietnam?
2. What does he see as the danger of "revisionism" of the Vietnam experience as a guide for interaction with other countries?

Thomas C. Fox, "Vietnam 'Revised'—American Arrogance Lesson Never Learned," *National Catholic Reporter*, March 11, 1983. Reprinted with permission.

The Vietnam war has crept back into the public forum in recent months. The Vietnam veterans finally got a memorial which reminds us that young men die in wars. There were articles last month marking the 10th anniversary of the signing of the Paris peace accords which, of course, only meant more war.

But the most interesting—and disturbing—aspect of this renaissance of interest is the effort being made, allegedly with a distance and dispassion now finally possible, to "revise" the lessons of the Vietnam war. The first major "revisionist" account appeared last year in book form entitled *Why We Were in Vietnam*, a work of Norman Podhoretz, who argued that a better understanding of the Vietnam experience could lead us to a stronger national commitment to the defense of freedom.

Vietnam "Revisions"

Podhoretz argued that U.S. intentions in Vietnam were selfless, if misdirected, and that it is now time we recognized the effort marked one of the high points, not low points, in U.S. history.

Since then, others with predilections similar to Podhoretz' have tuned in, and we are even beginning to read, as in the Feb. 13 *New York Times Magazine*, that the United States "was probably in a stronger position in Vietnam in 1972, just before the Paris peace accords, than at any previous point in the war." The implication, of course, was that we should have held out for better terms or even possibly continued the war which was beginning to go our way.

Personally, I am pleased when people show interest in Vietnam. I lived in Vietnam for nearly five years during the heaviest U.S. military involvement. I learned to speak the language and got to know the people. I feel fairly certain most Americans have not learned the lessons of the war. Some of these lessons are applicable today, especially in the midst of loose talk about reasserting American will around the world.

Before we march into some new conflict or get even more embroiled in El Salvador or Honduras, it might be worth taking a quick look at three lessons to come out of the war.

Failure to Understand Other Cultures

1. We fail miserably to understand the people, cultures and histories of other nations.

In the case of Vietnam, millions of lives would have been saved, for example, had we learned Vietnamese history and literature. The word "Viet Nam," for example, means "Southern People." The Vietnamese define themselves as those people south of China who fought for 1,000 years to win their independence from their giant northern enemy. The sense of Vietnamese nationalism grew out of this conflict. Vietnam's national heroes have always been those who led the resistance against outside invaders. Some 100 years

153

of French colonial rule reinforced the notion, and by the time the western powers allowed France back into Vietnam following World War II, the Communists and nationalists were one and the same force.

Eventually, they drove out the French in 1954, the year the United States decided to take their place.

Seen in this light, the American effort to set up a South Vietnamese government in 1954 was a precarious endeavor at best. And the American involvement was fatally doomed by 1965 when U.S. ground troops entered Vietnam on a large scale. Every U.S. soldier who set foot on Vietnamese soil reinforced the righteousness of the nationalist resistance.

Anti-Communism Not Enough

2. An anti-Communist ideology is insufficient as a base for building a popular government. And if that ideology is an implant by the United States, the puppets eventually get to pull the strings.

Maturity Needed

The real lesson of Vietnam cannot be that America will prevail anywhere if only we try hard enough—or at the other extreme, that we are doomed to defeat, whatever the place, time, or circumstance. The real lesson is that a great power must be mature enough to adopt practical and proportionate policies. We've got to be tough-minded, not simple-minded.

The New Republic, May 16, 1983.

The U.S. government formed and supported the South Vietnamese government from its inception, taking anti-Communist Catholics out of northern Vietnam and making them the nucleus of the new regime, although Catholics represented only 10 percent of the Vietnamese population. The Saigon government never really "won" the support of most Vietnamese. It was widely viewed as corrupt and dominated by the military, whom the Vietnamese do not respect. The government offered an anti-Communist structure built with a massive U.S. propaganda organization which preached the fear of a Communist take-over.

Government leader after government leader recognized he owed his position to U.S. policy, but also knew the Americans needed him to fulfill their own mission. So who was in control? The Americans were never in a position to insist on true reforms, the end to the hated corruption—however self-defeating. Astute Saigonese, perhaps recognizing the futility of the U.S. actions, developed a "take the money and run" attitude through much of the war. The entire U.S. effort was built on sand.

3. Might does not make right; might makes enemies.

Everything the Americans brought to Vietnam reeked of perceived superiority. The Vietnamese felt this condescension immediately and resented it. Few of the millions of Americans who came to Vietnam ever lived among the Vietnamese. All U.S. officials—those who needed to know most—lived in "little Americas," villas or compounds fenced in with barbed wire and defense posts.

The most blatant forms of racism were spawned in a "them against us" attitude shared by nearly every American. Little or no respect was ever shown by the foreigners to Vietnamese customs, traditions, religious beliefs or values. Everything the Americans had to offer, they assumed, was superior. "If only the gooks could learn to live like us—but, of course, gooks can't."

America brought its firepower, too. I once heard it suggested that 5,000 U.S. bullets were fired against each enemy shot. The notion sounds preposterous unless you were there.

The destruction was almost always one-sided: we had the helicopter gunships, the B-52s, the gatlin guns on the C-47s. Young American soldiers hunted, yes *hunted,* men, women and even children from helicopter gunships flying over "free-fire zones." What kind of government would allow a foreign force to establish a "free fire zone" in one's own nation?

U.S. artillery outposts, secure behind claymore mines and sandbags, were assigned quotas. Night after night they fired into the darkness every few minutes, sending random terror into the countryside.

The means of warfare, always appalling, grew less discriminating with each passing month. Until by the early 1970s the U.S. sent daily B-52 missions from Guam, carpeting central Vietnam and the Mekong delta with millions of tons of bombs. The Christmas bombing of Hanoi in 1972 was only the most visible manifestation of this arrogance of power.

Other Destruction

U.S. might showed up in other destructive ways: nearly one-third of the South Vietnamese population was eventually homeless and forced into refugee camps or squatters' huts near the cities. Young women were viewed as only a potential means of sexual gratification. The elderly, traditionally the source of wisdom in Vietnam, were ridiculed and stripped of authority. The Americans looked to the military leaders for Vietnam's new national leadership.

The payoffs for going along with the Americans were immediate material gains. Imported fans, refrigerators, Japanese Hondas, televisions, portable radios, tape decks, cigarettes and wines were all paraded before the Vietnamese in an effort to teach consumerism to the country. Unfortunately western individualism helped tear apart eastern collective, family-based values. Those Vietnamese who went along became not only misfits in a nation seeking an identity, but victims in their own land.

U.S. might literally pillaged Vietnamese society, a task made easier by blinding American arrogance. But this same blindness assured a U.S. defeat—and continues today in U.S. foreign policy.

Faulty Revisions

Those asking that we "revise" the lessons of the war never learned those lessons in the first place. They now refer to Vietnam syndrome, characterized by timidity in asserting U.S. military power. We need to stand up to defend freedom worldwide, they tell us. We need to be proud of our valiant efforts in Vietnam, they would have us believe.

But they are wrong. For precisely the blind national will, false national price and an unending belief in U.S. military power—that they wish to rekindle—led us into war and again could slip us into a senseless conflict.

Whenever I hear the call to stand up and march on behalf of freedom, I pause, remember Vietnam and ask, "for whom?"

"The real lesson of Vietnam is . . . that certain questions must be answered in the affirmative before U.S. forces should be employed in a combat role."

The US Should Act from Self-Interest

Al Keller Jr.

Al Keller Jr. is an American Legion Commander. In the following viewpoint he expresses his belief that the United States had the correct motives for being in Vietnam. However the nation's interests, capabilities, and commitment were not properly assessed before intervention was started. It is essential, he says, to evaluate these things before taking action to aid another country.

As you read, consider the following questions:

1. What are some of the differences Mr. Keller sees between Vietnam and Central America?
2. Mr. Keller says that in response to Vietnam, many Americans have retreated into isolationism. Why does he believe these people drew the wrong lesson from Vietnam, and why does he see isolationism as a danger?
3. What are the questions that Mr. Keller believes must be answered before the US decides how much and what kind of help it should give another country?

Al Keller Jr., "A Lesson of Vietnam," *The American Legion*, May 1983. Copyright 1983, The American Legion Magazine, reprinted by permission.

On this Memorial Day, as we turn our thoughts to the memory of those loved ones and friends who lost their lives in time of war, each of us fervently prays that such sacrifice will never again be necessary. Yet, even as we pray, we know there are mighty forces at work that would rob us of those freedoms purchased and preserved at such dear price.

At this moment, Soviet-supported guerrillas are terrorizing El Salvador in an effort to gain and then solidify a foothold in Central America. We're not talking about central Asia here, or central Africa, or even central Europe—we're talking about Central *America*, our own backyard. Moreover, we're talking about the vital security interests of the United States. Our government has publicly, clearly and repeatedly "drawn a line" on Communist aggression south of El Salvador. If that demarcation is not adhered to, it may one day be necessary to defend a line north of Mexico.

Yet, despite the seriousness of this situation, the hue and cry within our own borders is, "No more Vietnams!"

Simplistic Evaluation

El Salvador is not Vietnam. Too much is at stake for such a simplistic evaluation to prevail. And too great to be ignored are the differences between our interests in Central America and our interests in Vietnam. Aside from the geographical differences, the national security implications of a Communist presence in that tiny country are awesome indeed compared to such a presence in Vietnam.

That Communist presence would grant to the Soviet Union yet another strategic advantage within our own hemisphere. It would keep American attention riveted to our southern border, while seriously diminishing our ability to aid Western Europe, to respond to crises in the Mideast and to protect our interests in the Pacific.

As veterans who know the horror of war firsthand; as Legionnaires who are well acquainted with conditions that tend to make war inevitable; and as Americans who yearn for a world at peace, we agree, "There should be no more Vietnams"—no more abandonment of a nation seeking the opportunity for self-determination and left impaled on the sword of Communist domination and slaughter.

Media hype implies the United States unwittingly and unwisely escalated its involvement in Vietnam, first by giving military aid, then U.S. advisers, which led to U.S. combat involvement and, finally, to defeat and disaster. The corollary contention is the U.S. government lied to and misled its own people during the escalation, and the Vietnamese government and people allied with us were corrupt, undeserving and ungrateful.

The reality is that the objective of the United States in Vietnam was to prevent the imposition of a Communist government on the people of South Vietnam. Until the day that U.S. troops were withdrawn, we were successful in that mission despite widespread criticism at home, severe political constraints and a rash of publicity that inaccurately interpreted events. To a large extent, the South Vietnamese were also successful in their role until Congress cut off all military aid to the struggling government—an appeasement to American public opinion formed mainly on a basic lack of understanding of the significance of Southeast Asia.

Lessons for the US

Lessons? Yes, indeed, please take note:

1. Don't let our strategy depend on the cooperation of the enemy. He may not be willing to cooperate. Then what?

2. Strategy should encompass both external and internal elements and deal effectively with both or, failing that, tell you when to cut your losses or enlarge the arena.

3. Learn from the Soviets, who know something about it. The Brezhnev Doctrine explicitly takes into account both "external and internal forces." We need no Brezhnev Doctrine, but we do need to understand the external-internal nexus.

4. When tactics determine strategy, the result is, e.g., to send pilots over an *external* triple-canopy jungle where they can hit but little, while American soldiers are fed incrementally into an *internal* simulated insurgency meatgrinder. Result: Don't slide sloppily into the role of the last player to lose.

5. Be serious. The Communists play for keeps. There will be no replays. Options kept too long dissolve. Hang our public image on our actions; don't build our strategy around a PR image.

No more Vietnams? Amen!

National Review, April 17, 1981.

At the time of the American withdrawal, the insurgents had been defeated and contained, and the countryside was approaching a condition of normalcy. So, the historical record should correctly read that U.S. involvement in South Vietnam, though extremely costly in terms of human life, achieved its objective. That is, as of the time of the 1973 Paris peace treaty (which the North Vietnamese savagely violated in the final 1975 invasion) South Vietnam had been saved from the Communists and had a reasonable chance to evolve into a free and prosperous society.

So, when the alarmists cry "No more Vietnams," we must realize that what they are really saying is that our national security policy will never again permit the use of a U.S. military force in a foreign land. This retreat to armed isolationism would undermine U.S. leadership of the free world and give the Soviets a golden opportunity to dominate other lands.

Essential Questions

The real lesson of Vietnam is not that the United States must never again commit its might to the fight for freedom on a foreign shore, but that certain questions must be answered in the affirmative before U.S. forces should be employed in a combat role....

- Is there clearly a vital U.S. interest at stake?
- Does the United States have the capacity to achieve its objectives at a reasonable cost?
- Are the government, military forces and citizens we are to assist willing to shoulder their fair share of the burden?
- And, finally, can a consensus of support for U.S. policy be maintained or developed among the American people?

Even if all those questions can be answered "yes," we must still complete a final, critical step. We must analyze the array of options open to the United States in achieving its objectives. These, of course, can run the gamut from economic aid all the way to direct military involvement....

"No More Vietnams!"

Right now, allies and potential enemies alike are watching how we honor our commitment to El Salvador. They are assessing our resolve based on our strength of national character, collective will and adherence to stated principles. And, surely, they are wondering if the specter of Vietnam will be misinterpreted, thus preventing this great nation from fulfilling its role as the foremost champion of freedom.

I believe we will honor our commitments to the people of El Salvador. I am certain we have the national character to stand by our principles and continue in our role as leader of the free world, no matter what difficult decisions must be made....

These things having been done, all Americans will be able to proudly say of Central America, "No more Vietnams were fought there."

"Can it be that the greatest of the lessons of Vietnam is that as a guide to future individual and national conduct, it offers no guidance at all?"

Vietnam Offers No Lessons

Philip Gold

Philip Gold teaches history and public policy at Georgetown University. In the following viewpoint he discusses four issues related to United States involvement in Vietnam that are currently being reevaluated, and often revised, by scholars and policy makers. He says that the reevaluations are being done in different manners and with different motivations and often do not jibe with one another. He suggests that the multiple conclusions bring into question the possibility of a "lesson" from Vietnam that could guide the country's future conduct.

As you read, consider the following questions:

1. What are the four areas which Mr. Gold says are being reappraised?
2. What questions are being raised in each of these areas?
3. Why do you think Mr. Gold concludes that there may be no lesson to be drawn from Vietnam?

Philip Gold, "Vietnam: Doubts for the 80s," *The Washington Times*, January 24, 1984. CC The Washington Times, 1984; reprinted with permission.

It is said—and, by and large, believed—that something important is happening to the American understanding of the Vietnam War. What Norman Podhoretz once referred to as "deliverance from debate" — the post-1975 national silence on the meaning of the tragedy—has given way to a serious attempt at a new understanding: a somber, sober, more-in-sorrow, slowly coalescing middle view.

In point of fact, however, four separate reappraisals are under way, and though they deal with the same event, neither their methodologies nor their conclusions—nor the new questions they raise—coincide. It is, of course, possible to pick and choose among the four, according to one's private predilections or professional interests. But only as a sum do they offer the wider perspective that this country so desperately needs, if that ugly time is to be first understood, then mastered, and then laid to rest. The four reevaluations are:

1. The nature of the decision to intervene

Wartime and early postwar assessments ranged from raw imperialism through more traditional forms of hubris through quagmire through just war to divinely mandated (if all-too-humanly executed) crusade.

All have their elements of truth. But it is now reasonably clear that President Lyndon B. Johnson ordered the crucial escalations neither in a fit of anti-communist fervor nor in defense of palpably vital American interests, nor even with much hope of success.

Rather, he committed America to an Asian war in order to maintain the Great Society consensus at home—a consensus which, he apparently felt (taking his precedent from Harry S. Truman) could not survive the blow to American prestige that the loss of Vietnam would entail. In effect, America went to war in Asia for the sake of urban renewal and day-care centers at home, surely one of the more bizarre linkages in human history.

And if it be objected that Mr. Johnson merely inherited an "inevitable" commitment, perhaps that can best be answered by invoking a quote from Georges Clemenceau, France's World War I leader. When, at the signing of the Paris Peace Treaty, a German diplomat asked what Clemenceau thought history would say about all this, *le tigre* answered: "I do not know. But I do know that history will not say that Belgium invaded Germany."

The record stands. President Truman might have intervened, but didn't. President Eisenhower might have intervened but didn't. President Kennedy might have intervened, but didn't. President Johnson did, and for reasons peculiarly his own.

And now it must be asked: Would a man less determined to engage in massive social engineering at home, a man less determined to remake society and be worshipped for it, have led us so ineptly into war?

2. The conduct of the war itself

Since the early '70s, most military analysis has emphasized two major themes: structural deficiencies in the "American way of war" and excessively restrictive, Washington-imposed rules of engagement—errors which, in combination, made the war a perpetual assault on the wrong targets.

But it is now reasonably clear that the military, whatever its internal deficiencies and external constraints, came far closer to winning the war than seemed possible at the time. In a poignant moment, U.S. Army Col. Harry Summers once mentioned to a North Vietnamese officer that American troops had never sustained a major defeat in the field. True, the enemy replied, but not relevant.

Misleading Hindsight

In short, the Viet Nam analogy is really the Viet Nam fallacy. It is fallacious not just in the objective difference between the two situations, but in the way that indulgence of a false analogy can skew judgment. In general, foreign policy is better served by a conscious attempt to analyze each situation afresh, rather than by the wisdom of hindsight (which, of course, is really not wisdom at all). Soldiers, it has often been said, have the bad habit of waging the last war. Americans in their current fretting over El Salvador, are similarly afflicted. Across the political spectrum, there is no one who wants to re-experience in Central America the defeat of Indochina. From that, the left is tempted to conclude: Better not to fight at all, anywhere, ever again. The right concludes the opposite: Fight somewhere, soon, only this time, by God, win!...

To the extent that policymakers and spokesmen for both left and right can avoid historymongering, so much the better. There is a converse to Philosopher George Santayana's famous warning. "Those who cannot remember the past are condemned to repeat it." It is equally true that those who dwell obsessively on the past are prone to poor analysis, divisive debate, unconstructive criticism and bad decisions as they face the future. In short, they are doomed to ask the wrong questions, which can only yield the wrong answers.

Strobe Talbott, *Time*, February 22, 1982.

Why not? In part, this "irrelevance of victory" stemmed from the nature of the war itself. All the communists had to do was not lose for long enough, while America had to win in some definitive manner. So long as the enemy refused to acknowledge defeat, no final, World War II-style victory was possible. And, given the realities of North Vietnam, no such triumph could have been expected.

But the war still could have been brought to a satisfactory conclusion—a long-term remission, actually—had successive administrations not blinded themselves to the possibility by their infatuation with the theory and practice of micro-managed, micro-calibrated "limited" war. Historically, most wars have been fought for limited objectives. But they have been *fought,* not managed. In the American theory, however, actual combat served as a means of "signaling" resolve to the enemy, rather than as an end in itself. U.S. forces fought to induce a desired state of mind (i.e., willingness to negotiate) in the enemy: not to bring about that willingness through actual defeat. And thus the meaningless obsession with body counts and bombing starts and bombing pauses and all the rest.

Militarily meaningless, these were the managerial indices by which the United States blinded itself to the fact that the enemy acknowledged no limits save those imposed upon him by actual defeat: a defeat which, ironically, very nearly came about.

And now it must be asked: Would administrations less infatuated with theories of conflict management and micro-calibrated response have been better able to grasp the possibility of a reasonable level of victory, and then explain it to a people who had been asked, first to fight, and then not to win, and finally, not to care at all?

3. The conduct of the American people

If successive administrations chose to manage the war, rather than fight it, they also chose to manage public support, rather than arouse it. They failed. By their unwillingness to generate the domestic fervor necessary for war, they surrendered the moral high ground to that war's domestic opponents.

And yet, with notable exceptions, these were not the traditional kinds of anti-war forces. Recall the "movement" of the '60s: that bizarre congeries of radical chic, adolescent tantrum, sexual anarchy, pharmacological excess, rude self-righteousness, and moral flatulence. For far too long, the "movement" — that carnival superimposed upon a tragedy — has been relegated to the national attic of vaguely embarrassing memories, or else exploited as nostalgia.

But the questions it raises about national conduct in time of stress should not—indeed cannot—be permitted to remain unanswered. For the "movement" initiated an ongoing and potentially deadly change in the nature of American politics; it entailed the reduction of political discourse and action to the expression of purely individual emotional states—a new barbarism of the self-centered, the self-indulgent, the irresponsible.

Writing some years ago, James Fallows (Harvard '70) recalled how convenient it was that the morally correct action—draft evasion—also kept him and his friends alive. But more was involved than simple self-deluding expediency. As Peter Clecak suggests in *America's Quest for the Ideal Self,* political dissent has become a source of individual self-gratification and fulfillment: *and what one dissents about matters less than that one avail oneself of such opportunities.*

And now it must be asked: If it is indeed true that, during Vietnam, the Politics of Feeling Good about Yourself became the standard of war and peace . . . was this a fitting, a proper, an honorable response?

4. The meaning of defeat

The day Saigon fell, the world failed to end. The long-term effects of the defeat remain unclear. But, at the moment, one consequence seems both overpowering and omnipresent: something called "Vietnam Syndrome"—a constellation of anxieties which defines the limits of American activity on this planet.

And now it must be asked: should Vietnam be taken as a precedent for anything? Is not the greatest of its lessons its mindlessness, and does not the perpetuation of "Vietnam Syndrome" also perpetuate that mindlessness? From mistaken theories of war to inept administration to a protest movement which elevated moral narcissism to the status of an absolute, all that emerged from the Vietnam experience is its utter sterility.

And, of course, its pain: then, and now, and to come.

And now it must be asked: Can it be that the greatest of the lessons of Vietnam is that as a guide to future individual and national conduct, it offers no guidance at all?

Evaluating Sources of Information

A critical thinker must always question sources of information. Historians, for example, usually distinguish between *primary sources (eyewitness accounts)* and *secondary sources (writings or statements based on primary or eyewitness accounts, or other secondary sources.)* A diary written by a Vietnam War veteran describing his or her war experiences is an example of a primary source.

In order to read and think critically one must be able to recognize primary sources. However, this is not enough. Eyewitness accounts do not always provide accurate descriptions. Historians may find ten different eyewitness accounts of an event and all the accounts might interpret the event differently. They must then decide which of these accounts provide the most objective and accurate interpretations.

Test your skill in evaluating sources of information by completing the following exercise. Pretend you are living 100 years in the future. Your teacher tells you to write an essay about the causes of the growing American public opposition to US military intervention in Vietnam between 1965 and 1975. Consider carefully each of the following source descriptions. *First, underline only those descriptions you feel would serve as a primary source for your essay. Second, rank only the underlined, or primary sources, assigning the number (1) to the source you think would provide the most accurate and objective information. Assign the number (2) to the second most helpful source, and so on, until all the primary sources have been ranked.*

If you are doing this activity as a member of a class or group, compare your answers with those of other class or group members. Be able to defend your rankings. You may discover that others will come to different conclusions than you. Listening to the reasons others present for their rankings may give you valuable insights in evaluating sources of information.

Assume that all of the following sources deal with the broad topic of the growing opposition to US military involvement in Vietnam.

1. A book written by Senator J. William Fulbright, a prominent critic of US involvement in Vietnam and chairman of the US Senate Foreign Relations Committee until 1973

2. A national radio and television address by President Lyndon B. Johnson in 1964

3. A speech by Ho Chi Minh, leader of North Vietnam, in 1967

4. A taped interview in 1974 of a member of the US Army's Charlie Company, involved in the much publicized Mylai village killing of Vietnamese civilians

5. A book written in 1970 by Bernard Fall, a well known American scholar of Vietnamese culture

6. A book written in 1983 by Stanley Karnow, a journalist who reported from Vietnam and studied American involvement for decades

7. A book written in 1974 by a British journalist who is a scholar of Vietnamese culture

8. An essay written in 1975 by an American sociologist who specializes in the study of American social attitudes

9. A statement issued in 1968 by an American antiwar organization called Clergy and Laymen Concerned, detailing the reasons for its opposition to the war

10. The viewpoint by Congressman Thomas J. Dodd in the first chapter of this book

11. A novel written by a war veteran, published in 1985

Periodical Bibliography

The following list of periodical articles deals with the subject matter of this chapter.

Thomas J. Bellows

"Lessons Yet to be Learned," *Society,* November/December 1983.

Peter L. Berger

"Indochina and the American Conscience," *Commentary*, February 1980.

J. Duiker

"Avoiding Another Vietnam War," *USA Today*, April 1982.

Meg Greenfield

"A Lesson in Futility," *Newsweek*, March 5, 1984.

Charles Horner

"America Five Years After Defeat," *Commentary*, April 1980.

Irving Howe and Michael Walzer

"Were We Wrong About Vietnam?" *The New Republic*, August 18, 1979.

Paul Shannon interviews Noam Chomsky

"Have We Forgotten the Lessons of Vietnam?" *Witness*, July 1983.

Southeast Asia Chronicle

Special issue: "Vietnam Is Still With Us," Issue No. 85, August 1982.

John Spragens and Chris Jenkins interview David Marr

"Reinterpreting the Vietnam Experience," *Southeast Asia Chronicle*, August 1982.

Harry G. Summers Jr.

"Vietnam Reconsidered," *The New Republic*, July 12, 1982.

Is Central America Another Vietnam?

THE
VIETNAM
WAR

"*The fact is, there are parallels between the disaster in Southeast Asia and the way in which the U.S. is approaching the crisis in Central America.*"

The Comparisons Are Evident

Gene H. Hogberg

Gene H. Hogberg received his B.A. and M.A. from Ambassador College in Pasedena. He is World News editor for *The Plain Truth*, a magazine published by the Worldwide Church of God with a focus on human events and religion. In the following viewpoint, Mr. Hogberg emphasizes three important parallels between Vietnam and Central America that he believes should warn the United States of its fallibility.

As you read, consider the following questions:

1. What three parallels does Mr. Hogberg see between Vietnam and Central America?
2. What lesson does Mr. Hogberg draw from these parallels?

Gene H. Hogberg, "The USA Paralyzed by the Ghost of Vietnam," *The Plain Truth*, July/August, 1983. Copyright © 1983 Worldwide Church of God. All rights reserved.

The talk of "dominoes" falling one after another in Central America and the Caribbean haunts the memory of many in the United States.

Such language is painfully reminiscent of traumatic experiences in Southeast Asia where the United States suffered its first defeat in war and where indeed dominoes did fall—South Vietnam, Laos and Cambodia.

The urge in the U.S. Congress *not* to intervene directly in Central America, even though the stakes are so much higher, is strong.

Make no mistake. America's "pride in its power" was shattered in Vietnam. The tragic experience of Vietnam stalks the halls of Congress and the corridors of editorial offices throughout the land. Vietnam, editorialized the March 28, 1983, issue of *The New Republic*, "will continue for many years to weigh like a nightmare upon the foreign policy of the living. . . ."

The fact is, there are parallels between the disaster in Southeast Asia and the way in which the U.S. is approaching the crisis in Central America.

Disturbing Parallels

First of all, the United States today *has no overall regional strategy* for meeting the challenge—or, at least one that has a broad consensus of support. Second, Washington, as in the 1960s and 1970s, is neglecting to deal with the real opponent. And finally, as in Vietnam, the U.S. is seeking not to win but merely "not to lose" the struggle.

Regarding the first parallel, retired U.S. Air Force General T.R. Milton wrote in the March 1983 issue of *Air Force* magazine that in Southeast Asia, "we were concentrating on a place called South Vietnam, and there were maps to prove its borders existed. In real life the borders did not exist and Ho Chi Minh [North Vietnam's leader] knew it. He, unlike our intellectuals, did have a strategy, one designed to . . . [consolidate] all of Indochina—Vietnam, Cambodia, Laos—under Hanoi's rule. He must have had trouble believing his luck when we declared North Vietnam, Laos, and Cambodia out of bounds."

Similarly today, many insist that each insurrection in Central America arises spontaneously from local conditions and is unrelated to other eruptions in the region.

The insurgents themselves say otherwise. Earlier this year. El Salvador's guerrillas declared, via their Radio Venceremos station in Managua, Nicaragua, that they were part of a regional struggle. "We are and will continue to be friends of the people and governments of Cuba and Nicaragua and we're not ashamed of it. To the contrary, it makes us proud to maintain relations with these nations," Radio Venceremos said. "Our war is and will continue to be national, but . . . *we view our plans in the framework of a regional*

171

conflict in which there are interests of the people of Central America, the Caribbean and Latin America."...

Second, in Vietnam, according to Colonel Harry G. Summers, interviewed in the *New York Times Magazine* of February 13, 1983, "North Vietnam was the real opponent." In chasing after Vietcong guerrillas in South Vietnam, he reports "we were like a bull charging the toreador's cape."

"The result," he said, "was that the army got caught up in...search-and-destroy operations which cost the lives of many American soldiers, outraged public opinion and did not deal with the source of Communist strength—North Vietnam....The Communists controlled the tempo of the fighting."

Except for restricted air attacks the United States never seriously took the war to the North. Weapons and materiel flowed into North Vietnam and down the Ho Chi Minh trail into South Vietnam virtually unimpeded throughout the war.

Similarly today, Cuba remains a well-armed and fortified sanctuary supporting the Central American battle zones.

More Soviet arms poured into that bastion during the years 1981 and 1982 than at any other time since the Cuban missile crisis two decades earlier. And now, since December 1982, Nicaragua, too, has been declared "off limits" by the U.S. Congress. Arms will thus continue to flow from Cuba to Nicaragua and into El Salvador

Bob Sullivan, *The Worcester Telegram*. Reprinted with permission.

172

across a labyrinth of routes similar to the Ho Chi Minh Trail network.

Finally, in Vietnam, the United States, despite its enormous investments of men and materiel, sought not victory but simply to "bring the enemy to the bargaining table" for a negotiated settlement—the apparent aim of U.S. policy in El Salvador today.

The U.S. gave up direct involvement in Vietnam in January 1973. Then Congress, despite pledges of support, drastically cut military aid to South Vietnam—while the Soviet Union doubled its support. South Vietnam crumbled in April 1975.

Numerous Parallels

What is it that Central America has in common with Vietnam...?

God knows, there are parallels enough. In both cases, well-orchestrated international campaigns have focused mercilessly on the political and moral failings of the government. In El Salvador, as in Vietnam, the introduction of elections and reforms, the reduction of human-rights abuses and corruption have proved not to have much effect on the drumbeat of criticism. In El Salvador, as in Vietnam, Congress calls the U.S. commitment into doubt, undermining the confidence of vulnerable allies in our reliability and their viability. And as with Vietnam, doubt is continuously voiced about whether the government of El Salvador is morally worthy of American approval or even of survival.

Jeane J. Kirkpatrick, *Reader's Digest*, July 1983.

"What followed," reported former President Richard M. Nixon, "was one of the great tragedies of history. The 'liberators' brought ruthless tyranny.... There were no boat people before the communists took over. Now 110,000 fleeing their liberators have drowned in the China Sea. Hundreds of thousands have been tortured and killed in 're-education' camps. In Cambodia alone *over three million* have been murdered and starved to death...."

Americans thought they could simply walk away from the chain of horrors they helped unleash in far-off Southeast Asia by giving up the fight. They won't be able to walk away as easily from a similar upheaval in Central America. If Congressional critics, continues Mr. Nixon, "oppose the president's request [for aid] they can justify their action by proclaiming that they are preventing...another Vietnam. But they cannot escape the responsibility for what happens thereafter...."

Grave Dilemma

Former Secretary of State Alexander Haig, in an appearance before a Congressional committee in 1982, expressed his convic-

173

tion that "the American people will support what is prudent and necessary, provided they think we mean what we mean and that we're going to succeed, and not flounder as we did in Vietnam."

That is easier said than done, many observers believe. The fact is, the American public and its representatives, far from being convinced as to what to do, are hopelessly divided. The defeat in Vietnam shattered national unity on foreign affairs and in addition stripped the power of the President to act decisively in the face of perceived threats to national security.

The United States is caught between not wanting to intervene directly and "losing" El Salvador altogether; between not wishing to offend historic Latin sensitivities and seeing one domino topple after another—right up to the Rio Grande. . . .

U.S. political analyst George F. Will put the threat in stark terms: "Events in Central America are spinning rapidly toward a decisive moment in U.S. history. None of the fictions that were used to rationalize acceptance of defeat in Vietnam can be used regarding Central America. The threat there is close [and] clear. . . . There the United States will show—will learn—whether it is any longer capable of asserting the will a great power requires, or whether the slide in paralysis is irreversible."

"Lucid understanding of Central America is rendered impossible by the phantasmagoria of Vietnam."

Comparisons Paralyze US Policy

Steven Philip Kramer

Steven Philip Kramer teaches history at the University of New Mexico. He is currently in Washington as an International Affairs Fellow of the Council on Foreign Relations. In the following viewpoint Mr. Kramer states that the United States has never come to terms with its disastrous involvement in Vietnam. He believes that this prevents clear analysis of current foreign relations problems.

As you read, consider the following questions:

1. According to Mr. Kramer, how does the United States' handling of the defeat in Vietnam differ from the way many other countries have handled major defeats?
2. Why does Mr. Kramer think it has been so difficult for the US to come to terms with Vietnam?
3. Why does he think this is a damaging situation?

Steven Philip Kramer, "Vietnam Never Ended: The Defective Heart of US Policy," *Commonweal*, December 2, 1983. Reprinted by permission of The Commonweal Foundation.

The central problem of American foreign policy today is that America has never come to terms with the significance of the Vietnam war. No genuine national dialogue has taken place to clarify what happened in Vietnam. There is no common understanding of what Vietnam meant; there is not even a common myth on which we can agree. Instead, there are many mutually contradictory myths, held by different groups, embodied in the functioning of our major institutions. The contradictions between these mutually exclusive myths produce paralysis.

Many nations have suffered defeats more grievous. In 1870, an inept French government blundered into a war for which it was unprepared, was defeated militarily, and immediately collapsed. Efforts to continue the war by a provisional government came to naught, a civil war ensued, two of France's departments were lost to the Germans, a heavy indemnity imposed. Yet in the following decades Frenchmen assessed what had gone wrong, and from their reflections emerged a society both stronger and more democratic which survived the German onslaught of 1914.

Why has the United States not been able to come to terms with the Vietnam experience?

Short-Range Solution

One reason is that the short-range solution which spontaneously evolved to deal with the Vietnam trauma was silence. Vietnam had produced deep and conflicting passions, passions which had threatened to rend asunder the nation. These passions were to be left in peace. Vietnam was like a bad dream; one day we would wake and it would be forgotten. But the nightmare still clutches us in its embrace.

Secondly, the circumstances under which the war ended were equivocal.

The anti-war movement, which had attained massive proportions and come to represent the sentiment of the majority, never succeeded in forcing the government to accept its position. The U.S. never withdrew on the grounds that it should not have been in Vietnam; it withdrew because of "Vietnamization." The denouement of Vietnamization could hardly leave a good taste even in the mouth of the war's opponents. Moreover, the anti-war movement, heterogeneous though it was, had a general desire not only to end the war but also to reform the political and social structures believed to have brought it about. The McGovern candidacy was expected to at least initiate a thoughtful debate on the condition of America; the election instead turned into a rout; rather than the culmination of the movement, it proved its demise.

Likewise, those who favored continued support for South Vietnam were not convinced that our involvement was wrong, nor did the fall of Saigon, under the circumstances, convince them other-

wise. Many still thought the war should have been fought, others that if it was fought, it could and should have been won. The blood-bath in Cambodia, the harsh nature of the rule in "liberated" South Vietnam seemed proof to them that we had sacrificed a good cause to a bad, or at the very least, abandoned our friends to ruthless enemies.

Distrustful Reflexes

The reflexes born of Vietnam have come to permeate the work-ing of our political institutions. Vietnam began, and Watergate com-pleted, a process by which Congress, the press, and much of the American public came to doubt the sincerity of our presidents and worry about the concentration of power in the hands of the ex-ecutive. Similarly, they began to question whether the real threat to world peace came from the United States or from the Soviet Union, whether America's greatest contribution to world peace might not be simply to avoid involvement on foreign shores. In the aftermath of Vietnam, the making of foreign policy, necessarily the task of the executive but also a concern of Congress, had been undercut by generalized skepticism and distrust.

The problem will not be remedied by tinkering with the mechanism; no rules will stop leaks if even those who serve in government have lost faith in the institution.

We are now facing the problem of Central America. The way we deal with it will greatly influence the future of the hemisphere. Yet for many, lucid understanding of Central America is rendered impossible by the phantasmagoria of Vietnam. Proponents and opponents of our policy alike argue their case on the basis of Vietnam analogies, convincing no one because there is not one Vietnam analogy, but many. We shall not be able to deal rightly with Central America until we are able to deal with Vietnam.

"Virtually every element in the Indochina struggle is present in El Salvador."

The Communist Threat Creates the Parallel

M. Stanton Evans

A graduate of Yale University, M. Stanton Evans is a Washington-based journalist whose conservative opinions appear in newspapers nationwide. He has written several books including *The Future of Conservatism.* In this viewpoint, Mr. Evans defines a "Vietnam" and shows how El Salvador fits that definition.

As you read, consider the following questions:

1. In Mr. Evans' view, what is a "Vietnam"?
2. What difference does he see between El Salvador and Vietnam?
3. Why does he think El Salvador is "another Vietnam"?

M. Stanton Evans, "Why El Salvador Is 'Another Vietnam,'" *Human Events*, March 13, 1982. Copyright 1982. Reprinted with permission.

To determine whether or not El Salvador is in danger of becoming "another Vietnam," as we are so frequently instructed, we need to know what a "Vietnam" is.

On the historical record, the facts about the original Vietnam are pretty plain. The Communists in the North launched and sustained an ultimately successful war of aggression against the South, helped by plentiful supplies from outside Communist powers, most notably the Soviet Union. Similar wars were encouraged in neighboring Cambodia and Laos, with indigenous guerrillas prompted and aided by external forces.

War of Liberation?

The global "peace" movement and left-liberal cadres in our country treated all this as a "war of liberation," featuring the noble Ho Chi Minh against the repressive government in Saigon. Campus protests, marches and a ceaseless media campaign were mounted, demanding that we withdraw our support from the southern government. After a protracted struggle, this is exactly what we did.

When the armies of the North poured into Saigon and renamed it Ho Chi Minh City, and Cambodia went under to the Communists, the "peace" movement was ecstatic in welcoming the "liberation." In the aftermath, it turned out to be the opposite: Genocidal killings, brainwashing, forced labor, and suppression of religion rapidly ensued. One-third of the population of Cambodia was exterminated, while something like a million refugees fled Vietnam.

That, in rough outline, is what a "Vietnam" is. Do we have a similar situation brewing in El Salvador? The answer is an obvious "yes." Virtually every element in the Indochina struggle is present in El Salvador, beginning with the primal fact of attempted conquest by the Communists. The guerrillas in the country freely acknowledge their Marxist allegiance, while the flow of outside Communist aid and arms, from Moscow and Havana through the Marxist government in Nicaragua, has been well documented.

As President Reagan noted in his speech to the Organization of American States, a veritable flood of Soviet arms is pouring into the region: 66,000 tons of war supplies to Cuba in 1981, a Cuban fleet of more than 200 Soviet war planes, a horde of Soviets, Bulgarians, East Germans and North Koreans operating out of Nicaragua. Through Nicaragua, the President stated, "arms are being smuggled to guerrillas in El Salvador and Guatemala."

Marxist Threat

As occurred in Vietnam, left-liberal forces portray this as a homespun war of liberation, pitting freedom fighters of the left against a repressive oligarchy. Marches, protests and demonstrations are being staged once more, demanding withdrawal of U.S.

aid to the Salvadoran government. The media abound with charges against the anti-Communist regime.

Should this campaign succeed, it seems all too likely that El Salvador, too, will go under to the Marxists, with attendant holidays to celebrate the "liberation." Then we will find, to our infinite surprise, that the Marxists have imposed a brutal dictatorship, replete with executions, political prisoners, and repression of dissent.

Thus it has been not only in Vietnam but in numerous other countries "liberated" by the Communists: China, Cuba, Mozambique, Angola, Nicaragua. If the "peace" forces can work their will, there is every reason to suppose it will be that way in El Salvador, also: another nation sucked into the Marxist vortex, to the loud hosannahs of the "liberationists."

There are distinctions, of course. Vietnam is halfway around the world, while El Salvador is in our own backyard. We unwisely committed half-a-million Americans on the ground in Indochina, while no such commitment is contemplated in El Salvador, nor should it be. Most obviously, what is happening in El Salvador, and our reaction to it, are colored by the experience of Vietnam itself.

"WELL, IT SEEMS SENATORS DODD AND TSONGAS AND A COUPLE OF OTHER CONGRESSMEN DON'T WANT ANOTHER 'VIETNAM' IN EL SALVADOR... THEY SAY THE SIGNS ARE RIGHT FOR NEGOTIATIONS."

By Gary Brookins, *Richmond Times Dispatch*. Courtesy of News America Syndicate.

Boiling it down, a "Vietnam" is an attempted takeover of a country by local Communists, armed and prompted by the Soviet *apparat*, and abetted by people in the United States who do everything in their power to spread the propaganda of the Marxists and weaken the forces of resistance. At this writing, El Salvador seems an excellent candidate for such treatment.

> *"The president, while assuring us that El Salvador is not at all like Vietnam, nonetheless conjures the same image his predecessors did."*

Government Rhetoric Creates the Parallel

Ronald Steel

Ronald Steel is a senior associate at the Carnegie Endowment for International Peace. In this viewpoint he claims that El Salvador is not at all like Vietnam but that the kinds of statements the US government issues make it sould like the same kind of situation. It is this which creates the unfounded fears that involvement with El Salvador could turn into the same kind of quagmire that Vietnam was.

As you read, consider the following questions:

1. List the ways the author says that El Salvador is most definitely not like Vietnam.
2. What is the cause, according to Mr. Steel, of people fearing that El Salvador will be "another Vietnam"?
3. Does Mr. Steel believe that there is any threat to the well-being of the United States from the situation in El Salvador? Do you agree with him?

Ronald Steel, "Old Illusions Lead US to Make New Mistakes in El Salvador," *New York Times*, May 22, 1983. © 1983 by The New York Times Company. Reprinted by permission.

Is El Salvador just Vietnam closer to home? Clearly not. Vietnam was always part of another world. Its social structure, its customs, it language and religion were mysterious and impenetrable. It was either somebody else's colony (France's), or somebody else's sphere of influence (China's).

But El Salvador is another story. The Spanish language and Roman Catholicism are familiar. We have been involved there for a long time. It is part of "our" hemisphere. Like all nations around the Caribbean, and unlike Vietnam, it is within our "sphere of influence." That means we feel we have proprietary rights there.

El Salvador is just down the road from Mexico. Compared with the Viet Cong, the insurgents there are weak and isolated. They have no friendly giant on their border, as China was to Vietnam. With just a little more money and supplies, and perhaps a few more "advisers," we are told, they can carry the day. No American troops, of course. At least the president and his staff hope not.

They may be right. El Salvador is a tiny country. The guerrillas are outnumbered and outequipped. They have few modern weapons and no air force. This is not a full-scale civil war, like that in Vietnam, so much as a classic Latin American insurrection of peasants against soldiers. We have put down similar uprisings before, sometimes with our own forces. U.S. troops, after all, occupied neighboring Nicaragua until 1933.

Not Vietnam

No, El Salvador is not Vietnam. Yet the analogy keeps recurring. There is a deep feeling among the public and in Congress that this war, like the one in Vietnam, might drag on forever, sucking us in ever deeper. This arises not from the circumstances, which are very different, but from the pronouncements in Washington, which are remarkably similar.

The president, while assuring us that El Salvador is not at all like Vietnam, nonetheless conjures the same images his predecessors did. He asserts that this is a struggle between democracy and tyranny. He insists that we have a "vital interest" in the survival of the ruling regime.

Such sweeping statements bear scrutiny. First of all, democracy is not why we are supporting the government of El Salvador, any more than why we were in Vietnam. If our "friends" win, the country will remain a despotism ruled by landlords through the army. If the guerrillas take over, it will probably also be a despotism ruled by the army and a cadre of ideologues. In either case, democracy is not the issue.

Nor was it in Vietnam. To say that the Communist regime that now rules Vietnam is a vicious, nasty dictatorship is true. It is also irrelevant. How could it have been anything else? We did not go into Vietnam to bring democracy but to prop up a collapsing

regime. The same is true of El Salvador. Before the insurrection began, we cared no more about bringing democracy to El Salvador than we do today about bringing it to Chile. Let us please avoid hypocrisy and stop talking about democracy.

Vital Interests?

Let us then talk about interests. Do we have what the president calls a "vital interest" in El Salvador? If so, he has not made clear what that might be, any more than his predecessors did in the case of Vietnam. All during the long years of agony in Vietnam, we could never explain adequately, even to ourselves, why we were there.

One week it was to contain China, another to bring about the universal triumph of world law, and yet another to keep little yellowish-brown men from invading Akron and Missoula. It is not surprising that the consensus at home finally collapsed. The wonder is not that we fought the war for so long but that we didn't pick up and leave years earlier.

Our withdrawal from Vietnam did not result from weariness or a "failure of will," but from a realization that nothing that happened there was worth the sacrifices it involved. American security was not much affected by who ruled Vietnam. It is not today. There was no serious interest, let alone a vital one.

The same is true of El Salvador. It is an impoverished little country that does not endanger us regardless of who rules it. Whether it is a tyranny of the right or of the left need not overly trouble us.

184

Our involvement should be minimal.

While El Salvador is not Vietnam, the same illusions govern our policy toward it. If we have a "vital interest" in keeping the present regime in power, the president has not been able to demonstrate it. Until he does, we will be drawn ever deeper into a struggle we do not understand over issues we cannot explain.

"*It was not until the prolonged U.S. involvement in Indochina undermined automatic domestic support for the imperial enterprise that 'free elections' emerged as an important tool of empire management.*"

The Claim of Free Elections Is Propaganda

Frank Brodhead

Active in the anti-intervention and disarmament movements for many years, Frank Brodhead is retired editor of *Radical America* and the *Resist* newsletter. He now works for the Tenant Action Group in Philadelphia. Mr. Brodhead has recently written a book, *Demonstration Elections,* with Ed Herman. In the following viewpoint he expresses his belief that the so-called free elections held in Vietnam and now in El Salvador are actually political ploys by the United States.

As you read, consider the following questions:

1. How does the author define "demonstration election"?
2. According to Mr. Brodhead, how did the United States come to develop demonstration elections as a political tactic?
3. What parallels does Mr. Brodhead see between El Salvador and Vietnam?

Frank Brodhead, " 'Free Elections': Vietnam and El Salvador," *Indochina Newsletter,* March/April 1984. Reprinted with permission.

In 1963 General Maxwell Taylor told a congressional subcommittee: "Here [in Vietnam] we have a going laboratory where we see subversive insurgency . . . being applied in all its forms. On the military side . . . we have recognized the importance of the area as a laboratory." Thus during the Kennedy administration the "best and the brightest" applied themselves to Vietnam, attempting to create a theory and practice of counterinsurgency that would defeat peasant revolutionaries not only in Indochina but in other, increasingly troublesome Third World nations. The "lessons" learned by the bright boys of the Kennedy administration now dominate the strategy and tactics of U.S. intervention under Reagan. This is particularly true in Central America: The Green Beret training received by Guatemala's army in 1968 is used to slaughter tens of thousands of indigenous people in the mountains; a "pacification program" drawing directly on the Vietnam experience has been put in place in El Salvador; and the highly visible "search for peace" (inevitably accompanied, as it was in Indochina, by an escalation of military violence) is now underway in Central America. . . .

Demonstration Elections

We are concerned here to analyze one of the tools of counterinsurgency developed during the Vietnam era. This is the *demonstration election.* One of the earliest uses of this tactic occurred in Vietnam in September 1967, when the Johnson administration organized the electoral victory of the Vietnamese generals Thieu and Ky in an attempt to legitimize to an increasingly restive U.S. Congress and public the slaughter which we were conducting in Indochina in the name of self-determination. This investigation is not a mere academic exercise to "set the record straight," for the demonstration election in Vietnam is an immediate forerunner of the Salvadoran elections. . . .

A demonstration election is one whose purpose is only secondarily to select political leaders or even to ratify the political leaders chosen by the imperial overseer. The purpose of the demonstration election, rather, is to convince the citizens of the United States that this client government is freely chosen and that U.S. intervention in the client state is desired by the client state populace. It is one of the major vehicles through which the United States legitimizes to the home audience the expenditure of billions of dollars and thousands of lives in the slaughter of more thousands of lives in the defense of ephemeral U.S. "interests."

Preventing Free Elections

It is significant that such an exercise, a demonstration election, has become necessary in managing U.S. interests in the Third World. For it was not always so. The United States intervened in Central America prior to the Second World War with no thought given to "electing" a Somoza in Nicaragua. Indeed, the United States has frequently intervened in Third World countries to *prevent* a free election, as it did in Vietnam in 1956 and in El Salvador in 1961 and 1972. It was not until the prolonged U.S. involvement in Indochina undermined automatic domestic support for the imperial enterprise that "free elections" emerged as an important tool of empire management. Thus U.S. support for "free elections" has been *selective,* tending to support elections which ratify a candidate of our choice while opposing elections in which the outcome is problematic. . . .

The evolution of "free elections" as part of the U.S. intervention strategy in Vietnam can be seen in four critical instances:

1. In 1956 the United States refused to support the elections which had been scheduled at the Geneva Conference two years earlier and which were intended to reunify Vietnam. President Eisenhower noted in his memoirs that all informed observers expected Ho Chi Minh to win 80 percent of the votes if the elections were held as scheduled. The United States supported Diem in his refusal to participate; in doing so it demonstrated that its commit-

Congratulations! Your democratic elections qualify you for certain privileges . . . '

ment to "free elections" in Third World countries is good only when military occupation and pacification have proceeded to the point where elections are a safe bet.

Stacked 1966 Election

2. The tactical role of elections in U.S. pacification strategy can also be seen in the elections of September 1966. The massive U.S.

invasion and occupation of Vietnam that took place in 1965 and 1966 was opposed not only by the National Liberation Front (NLF) but also by organized Buddhist groups, which after the NLF constituted the largest political force in South Vietnam.... To quiet the opposition Ky (with U.S. support) promised elections for a Constituent Assembly. As the demonstrations receded Ky launched a full-scale military campaign against Danang and Hue, using U.S. planes and bases to occupy both cities by force. Hundreds of Buddhists were arrested and their organizations largely destroyed.

Having eliminated the only major political force in the South besides the NLF, the Ky regime then moved to hold elections. Despite a call by the Buddhists to boycott the election, the regime claimed that 80 percent of the eligible voters had turned out to elect an Assembly dominated by military personnel, civil servants, landlords, and Catholic refugees from the North. That is, despite the fact that both major political groups in the South were ineligible to participate in the election and that the Buddhists had urged an election boycott, the Johnson administration supported the election and claimed that it showed the United States was in Vietnam to promote freedom and democracy.

The 1967 Election

3. The presidential election of September 3, 1967 was a model demonstration election. Like the election in the previous year, it was held to pacify growing U.S. opposition to the war. By August 1967, for example, polls showed that only 33% of the U.S. public approved Johnson's conduct of the war. Thus the election was an opportunity to restate the public relations justification for U.S. presence in Vietnam: that we were supporting self-determination and democractic values. But the cynicism of these claims is evident if we compare the characteristics of genuinely free elections to the reality of the South Vietnam election of 1967:

• There was no freedom of speech in South Vietnam. "Neutralism" [favoring negotiation] was proscribed and candidates accused of "neutralism" were taken off the ballot by the Ky-dominated Assembly.

• The radio and TV in South Vietnam were controlled by the government. The government also censored and effectively controlled the privately owned press....

• We have already noted that organizational freedom was nonexistent in South Vietnam. Neither the NLF nor the organized Buddhist groups could participate in the election.... Thus no effective opposition was allowed in this "free election."

• State terror had reached a high level in South Vietnam by 1967. The jails were filled with thousands of political prisoners. Members of the Assembly who opposed Thieu-Ky were the subject of death threats. Peasants also knew that voting and voting right were necessary to stay alive; members of the South Vietnamese national police were stationed inside and outside the polling places. As a former Saigon official told one U.S. analyst: "...If an individual was found without the election-day stamp on his registration card it meant prison and in some cases even death. The real meaning of the election was not lost on the people. They voted to stay out of jail. They also knew from past experience that the government-picked candidates would win regardless of how they voted."...

The Pentagon Papers...reveal that the election had the purpose not of ending the Vietnam conflict but of clearing the ground for further escalation, "in which maximum military pressure must be maintained" on the enemy. The purpose of the election was to rally another round of support within the United States for the continued military effort in Vietnam. "Self-determination" was what the election was engineered to prevent, not what it was meant to achieve.

Farcical Election

It is difficult to say which was more absurd: the chaotic March 25 election in El Salvador or the U.S. attempt to extol it as an example of democracy in action.

So intent is the United States on scoring a propaganda victory—on covering an oppressive and bloody military regime with a veneer of "freedom and democracy"—that U.S. officials hailed the election even though it was a self-evident farce....

The administration and Congress shamelessly peddle this fraud as justification for continued support for an unspeakable regime....

Behind that smoke screen, the United States continues to back a military regime that viciously represses the Salvadoran people, that has murdered one percent of them in the last five years, and that denies them any chance at self-determination. It does this on behalf of U.S. and Salvadoran ruling-class interests, which have combined to make El Salvador one of the world's most impoverished countries.

The People, April 14, 1984.

---

4. It is ironic that our fourth South Vietnamese election, that of 1971, could have advanced U.S. interests if the United States would have allowed a genuinely free election to take place. Seymour Hersh points out in his study of Kissinger *(The Price of Power)* that by 1971 the North Vietnamese were ready to settle the war with a mutual withdrawal of forces, a prisoner exchange, and an Indochina-wide ceasefire, if the United States would allow a free election in South Vietnam. The North Vietnamese believed that an election held under conditions of U.S. neutrality—i.e. not intervening to manipulate the reelection of Thieu—would result in

the emergence of a non-Communist but neutralist regime under a moderate like General Minh. They were prepared to live with this if it would end the war. But Nixon and Kissinger refused to take such a neutral stance in the election, investing millions of dollars in Thieu's reelection. This ended negotiations between the United States and North Vietnam and began four more years of brutal warfare. . . .

The parallels between the U.S. use of "free elections" in Vietnam and the 1982 demonstration election in El Salvador are striking. In both instances the U.S. media presented the demonstration election as a real exercise in democracy, not a tactic of intervention. In neither case were the long- or short-term violations of the conditions we outlined above for a genuinely free election explored by the media. In both elections long lines of peasants waiting to vote were interpreted not as an instance of coercion and fraud, but as a sign of the peasants' desire for peace and the U.S.-sponsored regime's commitment to self-determination. And in neither case did the media analyze how such a "vote for peace" could become the cause for further escalation of the war.

El Salvador and Vietnam

As we approach another demonstration election in El Salvador, the 1967 election in South Vietnam assumes a particular relevance. For as Kahin and Lewis noted in their history of Vietnam, this election marked a turning point which set U.S. policy on a murderous course. "With the election over," they noted, "President Johnson could now assure the American public that the sacrifices they were making in Vietnam were in support of a 'legitimate,' freely elected government representing the will of the South Vietnamese people. However farcical the election appeared at the time, henceforth Washington in defending its policies would refer to 'the elected government of South Vietnam.' The opportunity for effectively broadening the base of the Saigon regime had been lost. Whatever leverage it gained in dealing with opposition to the war in the United States, the Johnson Administration was now tied even closer to the Thieu-Ky leadership." (*The United States in Vietnam* [Revised Edition], p. 359) This analogy will be complete when the Reagan administration justifies U.S. intervention in Central America on the ground that it was invited to intervene by the freely elected government of El Salvador. In evaluating U.S.-sponsored "free elections," therefore, we will do well to learn and publicize the effect that such elections had in legitimizing and perpetuating the U.S. invasion of Vietnam.

"The institutions of democracy in Central America are uncertain, but the idea of democracy is not. The Salvadoran elections. . . are proof."

Free Elections Serve Democracy

The New Republic

The New Republic is a weekly journal of opinion that focuses on politics and literature. In the following viewpoint, the editors of *The New Republic* state that the supposed parallels between Vietnam and El Salvador distract policymakers from thinking clearly about how best to help the situation in Central America. They contend that the United States *must* help: The free elections held in El Salvador, far from being examples of US manipulation, prove the desire for a democratic society there.

As you read, consider the following questions:

1. Why does the author think that the Vietnam analogy is not helpful?
2. How does the author think the United States can best help in Central America?
3. What do the authors say the Salvadoran elections prove?

"How to Help El Salvador," *The New Republic*, March 28, 1983. Reprinted by permission of *The New Republic*, © 1983, The New Republic, Inc.

Damn Vietnam. It is now entering its third decade of interference with America's perception of America's interest. In the 1960s it beckoned us into a blunder, which was to involve ourselves in a revolutionary situation that was of little consequence to the United States. In the 1980s it beckons us again into a blunder, which is to absent ourselves from a revolutionary situation that may be of considerable consequence to the United States. The President has asked for $60 million more in military aid to El Salvador. His request has provoked a debate that seems to be less about Central America than about Indochina. Mr. Reagan assures us that "there is no parallel whatsoever with Vietnam," while an unidentified member of the State Department says that "what we're talking about here . . . is a Vietnamization of the process." And the press and the pundits address themselves portentously to the collective memory. "Why Are We in Vietnam?" asks Anthony Lewis about El Salvador. (He also has the impertinence to write of the present Salvadoran government that it "shot its way in," when the only shots that were fired when this government came in were fired by guerrillas—and at voters.)

Important Differences

Well, we are not in Vietnam, and we are barely in El Salvador. Whether we should be in El Salvador—the how and the why of our relationship to Central America in general—is a great public question. It will not be answered by political necromancy. When the past is an obsession it gives no instruction. The differences between El Salvador and Vietnam are at least as important as the similarities. Among these differences are many thousands of miles. It is not irrational for the United States to want the Soviet Union out of its neighborhood, though it is irrational for the United States to believe that only guns will keep the Soviet Union out. Naturally it is difficult for us to escape the encrustations of the recent past. Vietnam will continue for many years to weigh like a nightmare upon the foreign policy of the living. But we must make our foreign policy in a waking state. The task before the American government is not simply to stay out of Vietnam. It is to provide security for the United States in a manner that will not preclude social justice in El Salvador. . . .

What should the American objectives in El Salvador be? There are those who think that this is a great new opportunity for American isolationism, that all we should send to El Salvador are our regrets. There are others who think that there is nothing wrong with El Salvador that a military victory cannot cure. We disagree with both groups. Handing the country over to the Leninists along the Lempa would damage El Salvador and the United States, and so would destroying the country in the attempt to liquidate them. It seems obvious that El Salvador has both a military and a political

193

problem, which require both a military and a political solution. . . .

Obviously there is a political problem in El Salvador, too, and it will not be solved by military means. The political problem is the result of fascism and poverty, of a right-wing repression and an oligarchic economic reality. The defeat of the guerrillas will remove neither. The Soviet threat is a bad excuse for both.

Heroic Elections

While elections of and by themselves will not solve all problems, they are another important step forward on the difficult path toward democracy. . . .

We often forget that democracy requires heros—the silent heros who believe that ballot boxes, not bullets, resolve issues and stand the test of time. El Salvador will face a serious and important test on March 25. Our own faith in democracy should lead us to believe that, in spite of all the challenges, El Salvador will emerge stronger, surer, and reconfirmed in its determination to advance the course of peace and democracy.

Thomas R. Pickering, address, March 1, 1984.

The answer to the repression in El Salvador is free elections with the widest possible participation, and the simultaneous withdrawal of any and all American support from the repressors themselves. The Reagan Administration appears to have disabused itself of the idea that Roberto D'Abuisson and his gang can represent our interests. We were edified by the Administration's backing of President Magaña and Defense Minister José Guillermo Garcia during their recent struggle with "Mr." D'Abuisson. Who, then, should the United States support? The center, we liberals say, and say again. But we must understand what a center is and who a center is. A center will not abandon the war against the guerrillas, it will not collectivize the economy, it will not secede from the competition between East and West, it will not set out to remake man. A center is a center, not a left. This is particularly true in El Salvador, where the center is constituted by the Christian Democrats. Since the 1960s, when Christian Democracy took root throughout Latin America, the Salvadoran moderates have developed a position characterized by constitutionalism, economic growth, trade unionism, a strong belief in property, anticolonialism, anti-Castroism—all with a decidedly Catholic coloration.

The center has traditionally been a creation of the middle class, and the Christian Democrats of El Salvador are no exception. They came upon the scene as the political and intellectual corollary of the successful industrialization of some of the Salvadoran economy.

(José Napoléon Duarte, who carries the flag, is an engineer.) This is the good news and the bad. The industrialization of the Salvadoran economy did not go very far; the economy remains overwhelmingly agricultural. Moreover, the urban middle class, the "coffee bourgoisie" whose prosperity was based upon the unfair distribution of the land and the unjust treatment of the agricultural laborers. The Christian Democrats, in other words, are only a part of a small part of Salvadoran society. As in geometry, the center is the point around which things revolve, but it does not take up much space.

Elections Proof of Democracy

All is not lost, however. The institutions of democracy in Central America are uncertain, but the idea of democracy is not. The Salvadoran elections last March are proof. The Christian Democrats, furthermore, are not without possible allies in the attempt to hold a free election. There exists in El Salvador, as elsewhere, a coincidence of interests and ideals between the right wing of the left and the left wing of the right. José Napoléon Duarte has more in common with Guillermo Ungo than with Roberto D'Abuisson. This is where "dialogue"—as it is gingerly known—comes in. While negotiations with the guerrillas for their admission to power must be ruled out, "dialogue" with the democrats among them must not. As U.N. Ambassador Jeane Kirkpatrick observed recently, whoever wishes to participate in the democratic process must be approached. (She might also have observed that the United States will do all it can to protect the safety of those who do.)

And Mrs. Kirkpatrick had another good idea—a Marshall Plan for Central America. "The Marshall Plan," she said, "constituted a response to a regional problem that was simultaneously economic and social and military." That is precisely what American policy in El Salvador should be—a policy on many tracks. A meaningful program for the redistribution of land will do more to keep Castro out than any White Paper we can produce. Recently the Salvadoran assembly voted to extend the present program by ten months—and over the objections of the right. It was a small thing, but it was a good thing. If the United States were to throw its weight behind it, it would be a great thing.

Reforms for Stability

Free elections, "dialogue" with all of Salvador's democrats, military assistance, pressure for the observance of human rights, agricultural reform, economic renewal—and all in the middle of a civil war. . . .

Global threats are made up of regional instabilities. Castro did not create the cracks in Central American society; he found them, and tried to make use of them. Heal these cracks—create the social

195

and economic conditions in which democrats will not despair and make alliances with enemies of democracy—and destroy the death squads as you destroy the guerrilla cells—and the East will have lost another avenue to the West.

Lessons to Be Learned from Vietnam

It is said that experience is life's best teacher. However, one must actively reflect on past experiences to derive lessons for the present and future. The purpose of this activity is to examine the reason for America's failure in Vietnam and to see if there are lessons to be learned that can be helpful in directing America's foreign policy toward Central America.

Part 1

Step 1.   The class should break into groups of four to six students. Working individually within each group, each student should rank the reasons listed below for America's failure in Vietnam. *Assign the number 1 to the reason most responsible for American failure, the number 2 to the second most important reason, and so on, until all the reasons have been ranked. Add any reasons, not listed, that you think should be included.*

Step 2.   Students should compare their rankings with others in their group, giving the reasons for their rankings.

Reasons for America's Failure in Vietnam

1. US failure to declare war
2. Unexpected determination of the enemy
3. US peace movement that undermined public support
4. Russian & Chinese support of the enemy
5. Lack of US determination
6. Critical press accounts that undermined public support
7. Poorly planned US military strategy
8. Incompetence of US political leaders
9. An unjust cause

10. Lack of support by America's allies
11. Lack of support of the South Vietnamese people
12. _____
13. _____
14. _____

Part 2

Step 1.   Each small group should draft a *Statement of Vietnam Lessons* that current US leaders should study in planning American policy toward Central America. Include a minimum of four lessons in each draft.

Lesson 1. _____

_____

Lesson 2. _____

_____

Lesson 3. _____

_____

Lesson 4. _____

_____

Step 2.   Each small group should compare its draft and rankings from Part 1 with others in a classwide discussion.

Step 3.   The entire class should draft a *Statement of Vietnam Lessons*. Include a minimum of six lessons in the classwide draft.

Step 4.   Send a copy of the classroom draft to appropriate government officials:

    the President of the United States
    the two US senators representing your state
    your congressman or congresswoman
    the US Secretary of State
    the US Secretary of Defense
    others the class considers appropriate

198

Periodical Bibliography

The following list of periodical articles deals with the subject matter of this chapter.

Robert J. Bresler — "Vietnam and Central America: Reflections on Power and Morality," *USA Today*, September 1983.

M. Stanton Evans — "Central America, The Limited War Game, How to Make Another Vietnam," *Conservative Digest*, June 1983.

The Heritage Foundation — "Central America and the Lessons of Vietnam," September 1983. Pamphlet available from The Heritage Foundation, 214 Massachusetts Avenue NE, Washington, DC 20002.

Jeane J. Kirkpatrick — "Will El Salvador Go the Way of Vietnam?" *Human Events*, March 5, 1983.

Robert A. Kittle — "Heading for Another Vietnam," *U.S. News & World Report*, March 21, 1983.

Peter R. Kornbluh — "US Involvement in Central America: A Historical Lesson," *USA Today*, September 1983.

The New Republic — "Choices in Central America," May 16, 1983.

The New Republic — "The Vietnam Analogy," March 17, 1983.

Robert A. Pastor — "Our Real Interests in Central America," *The Atlantic Monthly*, July 1982.

Strobe Talbott — "El Salvador: It is Not Vietnam," *Time*, February 22, 1982.

Stephen B. Young — "Salvador Parallels Vietnam: This Time, Let's Win," *The New York Times*, May 22, 1983.

Chronology of US Involvement in Vietnam

1930	The Indochinese Communist Party is formed under the leadership of Ho Chi Minh and joins the resistance to French colonial rule.
1940	Japanese occupy Indochina but permit French administration to continue.
May 8, 1941	Ho Chi Minh forms the Viet Minh to fight the French and the Japanese.
August 18, 1945	Viet Minh takes control of Vietnam.
September 2, 1945	Ho Chi Minh announces the foundation of the Democratic Republic of Vietnam (DRV).
September 13, 1945	British forces arrive in Saigon to begin disarmament of the Japanese and to assume control of Vietnam.
September 26, 1945	Lieutenant Colonel A. Peter Dewey is the first American to be killed in Vietnam.
December, 1946	Viet Minh attack French positions and the Franco-Vietnamese war begins.
June, 1948	Bao Dai becomes chief of state of Vietnam under French control.
July, 1949	Bao Dai decrees the establishment of the State of Vietnam.
January 14, 1950	Ho Chi Minh proclaims the Democratic Republic of Vietnam as the only legal government of Vietnam.
January 18, 1950	China recognizes the DRV as the legal government of Vietnam.
February 7, 1950	The United States and Britain recognize Bao Dai's government.
June 27, 1950	President Truman announces military aid to French forces and the sending of a military mission to Vietnam.
December 23, 1950	A Mutual Defense Assistance Agreement is signed by the United States, Vietnam, France, Cambodia and Laos.
May 7, 1954	French are defeated at Dien Bien Phu by Viet Minh forces.

June 16, 1954	Bao Dai selects Ngo Dinh Diem as prime minister of the State of Vietnam.
July 21, 1954	Geneva Conference calls for a cease fire in Vietnam and divides it at the seventeenth parallel. Ho Chi Minh assumes control of North Vietnam and Bao Dai rules South Vietnam. Bao Dai's government denounces the agreement and the United States declines to sign it.
September 8, 1954	The Southeast Asia Treaty Organization (SEATO) is formed by the United States, France, Britain, Australia, New Zealand, Pakistan, Thailand and the Philippines.
January 1, 1955	United States begins to send aid directly to the Saigon government.
February 12, 1955	US advisory group begins to train the South Vietnamese army.
October 26, 1955	Diem, after defeating Bao Dai in a referendum, announces the Republic of Vietnam and himself as president.
May 8-19, 1957	President Diem visits US, addresses a joint session of Congress and receives a declaration of support from President Eisenhower.
May, 1959	US advisors are ordered to Vietnam to assist South Vietnamese infantry, artillery, armored and marine forces.
December 20, 1960	National Liberation Front (NFL) is formed in South Vietnam with Hanoi's support to overthrow the Saigon government.
May 5, 1961	President Kennedy announces it may be necessary to send US troops to Vietnam.
December 8, 1961	US State Department publishes "white paper" claiming that South Vietnam is threatened by "clear and present danger" of communist aggression.
February 7, 1962	Two US Army air support companies arrive in Saigon, bringing total of US troops in South Vietnam to 4000.
February 24, 1962	China demands a withdrawal of US troops from Vietnam, claiming its security is threatened.
May 8, 1963	Rioting, which lasts several months throughout South Vietnam, breaks out on Buddha's birthday between Diem's government and antigovernment demonstrators.

August 24, 1963	Washington recommends President Diem be removed in a cable to Saigon Embassy.
November 1, 1963	Military coup overthrows Diem government, killing Diem.
November 22, 1963	President Kennedy is assassinated.
November 23, 1963	President Johnson announces continued US support of South Vietnamese government.
January 30, 1964	Military coup by General Khanh overthrows government of General Minh.
June 12, 1964	French President Charles de Gaulle calls for an end to all foreign involvement in Vietnam.
July 19, 1964	General Khanh and Air Marshall Nguyen Cao Ky call for air strikes against North Vietnam.
August 2, 1964	US destroyer Maddox is attacked in Gulf of Tonkin by North Vietnamese torpedo boats.
August 4, 1964	US destroyers Maddox and Turner Joy are attacked by North Vietnamese PT boats and President Johnson orders retaliatory air raids against North Vietnam.
August 7, 1964	Tonkin Gulf Resolution is passed by Congress (88-2 in Senate and 416-0 in House) giving President Johnson the authority to use "all necessary steps, including the use of armed force" in Southeast Asia.
February 7, 1965	President Johnson orders bombing of North Vietnam after eight Americans are killed in a Viet Cong attack.
February 27, 1965	State Department issues "white paper" accusing North Vietnam of aggression.
March 8, 1965	First US combat troops land at Da Nang.
April 7, 1965	President Johnson offers a $1 billion Southeast Asia aid package if North Vietnamese will participate in "unconditional discussions."
June 8, 1965	State Department publicly authorizes US troops to participate in combat.
October 15-16, 1965	Nation-wide demonstrations in the US sponsored by the National Coordinating Committee to End the War in Vietnam.
April 12, 1966	B52s bomb North Vietnam for the first time.
October 25, 1966	US offers to withdraw troops six months after Hanoi withdraws its forces.

January 10, 1967	President Johnson requests 6% income tax surcharge to finance Vietnam involvement.
April 15, 1967	100,000 demonstrate against the war in New York and San Francisco.
April 3, 1968	North Vietnam offers to participate in peace talks.
October 31, 1968	President Johnson halts bombing of North Vietnam.
May 14, 1969	President Nixon proposes simultaneous withdrawal of US and North Vietnamese troops.
June 8, 1969	President Nixon announces first US troop withdrawal of 25,000 men.
July 25, 1969	President announces "Nixon Doctrine" calling for replacing US combat troops with economic and military aid.
September 3, 1969	Ho Chi Minh dies.
October 15, 1969	Hundreds of thousands participate across US in Vietnam Moratorium demonstrations.
November 3, 1969	President Nixon appeals to the "silent majority," claiming withdrawal from Vietnam would harm US interests.
November 12, 1969	US Army announces alleged killing of over 100 civilians by US troops in March of 1968 in village of My Lai.
April 29, 1970	US troops invade Cambodia to attack North Vietnamese and Viet Cong sanctuaries.
May 4, 1970	Ohio national guardsmen kill four Kent State University students during anti-war demonstration.
June 24, 1970	Senate repeals 1964 Gulf of Tonkin resolution by a vote of 81 to 10.
March 29, 1971	Lt. William L. Calley convicted of murdering South Vietnamese civilians at My Lai.
June 13, 1971	*The New York Times* begins publication of *The Pentagon Papers*.
January 25, 1972	President Nixon reveals that Henry Kissinger, his national security advisor, has been engaged in secret Paris peace talks since August 1969.
May 8, 1972	President Nixon announces the mining of North Vietnamese harbors.
August 12, 1972	Last US combat troops leave Vietnam.

January 23, 1973	President Nixon announces agreement has been reached for "peace with honor."
January 27, 1973	Cease-fire agreement signed in Paris and Secretary of Defense Laird announces end of military draft in US.
March 29, 1973	American POWs leave Vietnam along with remaining US troops.
April 23, 1975	President Ford announces the war "finished."
April 30, 1975	General Ming surrenders Saigon to Communists and remaining Americans are evacuated.
January 21, 1977	President Carter pardons most Vietnam war draft evaders.
November 11, 1982	Vietnam veterans memorial dedicated in Washington, D.C.

Annotated Bibliography

Books

Asia Society

Vietnam: A Teacher's Guide. New York: The Asia Society, 1983. Helpful 28-page booklet for teachers or students designed to accompany the PBS television series *Vietnam: A Television History*, but contains material that is independently useful. Available from The Asia Society, 725 Park Avenue, New York, NY 10021.

Mark Baker

Nam. New York: Quill, 1982. Graphic descriptions of the war in short statements by those who fought. Very powerful.

Larry Berman

Planning a Tragedy: The Americanization of the War in Vietnam. New York: W. W. Norton, 1982. Presents the view that American involvement was based in large part on President Johnson's attempt to appease conservative legislators and save his "Great Society" legislation.

Philip Caputo

A Rumor of War. New York: Holt, Rinehart & Winston, 1977. Moving personal account of a young Marine officer in his first, disillusioning, year of battle.

Steve Cohen

Vietnam: Anthology and Guide to 'A Television History.' New York: Alfred A. Knopf, 1983. Excellent collection of documents and articles with commentary by the editor covering the French/Indochina struggles through American withdrawal and consequent "legacies." Useful bibliographies, maps, photos.

Department of State

Foreign Relations of the United States 1952-1954, two volumes. Washington, DC: Department of State. Collection of documents, memos, speeches, etc. Excellent source for research on the beginnings of US involvement.

W. D. Ehrhart

Vietnam Perkasie: A Combat Memoir. McFarland, 1984. A penetrating look into the life of the ordinary soldier.

Frances Fitzgerald

Fire in the Lake. Boston: Atlantic-Little, Brown, 1972. Explains the US failure in Vietnam in terms of the cultural gap between the Vietnamese and Americans.

J. William Fulbright — *The Arrogance of Power.* New York: Random House, 1966. Prominent war opponent presents his case.

Leslie H. Gelb and Richard K. Betts — *The Irony of Vietnam: The System Worked.* Washington, DC: The Brookings Institution, 1979. Presents the view that the American military did its job but timid presidents were not committed to victory.

Allan E. Goodman — *The Lost Peace: America's Search for a Negotiated Settlement.* Stanford, CA: Hoover Institution Press, 1978. Claims a diplomatic solution was improbable because of Hanoi's commitment to total victory.

Mike Gravel, editor — *The Pentagon Papers,* five volumes. Boston: Beacon Press, 1971. The formerly secret documents from both Washington and Saigon documenting American involvement up to 1968.

Graham Greene — *The Quite American.* New York: Penguin Books, 1962. Classic novel of a naive American, adrift in Vietnam, guided by the ideological force of anti-communism.

David Halberstam — *The Best and the Brightest.* New York: Random House, 1972. Vivid sketches of the policymakers in the Kennedy-Johnson years and insight into their perceptions of Vietnam.

Michael Herr — *Dispatches.* New York: Avon, 1980. Highly acclaimed impressionistic account of the war from the vivid perspective of the journalist-author and the soldiers in the field.

George C. Herring — *America's Longest War.* New York: John Wiley & Sons, 1979. The views of a liberal anti-war critic.

Stuart A. Herrington — *Silence Was a Weapon: The Vietnam War in the Villages.* Novato, CA: Presidio Press, 1982. Experiences of an American military advisor in a South Vietnamese province.

A. D. Horne, editor — *The Wounded Generation: America After Vietnam.* Englewood Cliffs, NJ: Prentice-Hall, 1981. Anthology of first-hand articles by prominent writers about the war. The book is centered around a round-table discussion between the writers who recount combat experience, draft evasion, and the impact of the war on America.

George McTurnan Kahin and John W. Lewis
The United States in Vietnam, revised edition. New York: Dial Press, 1969. Offers a Vietnamese context for challenging the assumptions underlying US policy in Vietnam. The authors are students of Asian history.

Stanley Karnow
Vietnam: A History. New York: Viking, 1983. Companion volume to the 13-part PBS documentary television series. One of the most comprehensive books available on the war.

Paul M. Kattenburg
The Vietnam Trauma in American Foreign Policy, 1945-75. New Brunswick, NJ: Transaction, 1980. Explores America's involvement with Vietnam and how that involvement affected US foreign policy beyond the war itself.

Douglas Kinnard
The War Managers. Hanover, NH: University of Vermont, University Press of New England, 1977. The results of a survey of more than 100 army generals who commanded in Vietnam.

Henry Kissinger
The White House Years. Boston: Brown & Co., 1979. Covers the period 1969-1973. Memoirs of the former National Security Advisor to President Nixon and Secretary of State in the Nixon and Ford Administration.

Michael T. Klare
Beyond the "Vietnam Syndrome": US Interventionism in the 1980s. Washington, DC: Institute for Policy Studies, 1981. Discusses the impact of the "Vietnam syndrome" on policy and how it has affected our current interactions with Third World countries.

Ron Kovic
Born on the Fourth of July. New York: McGraw-Hill, 1977. Touching memoir of young patriot who not only becomes disillusioned but becomes a paraplegic as a result of his Vietnam service.

Daniel Lang
Patriotism Without Flags. New York: Norton, 1974. Celebrates the Americans who resisted the war.

Guenter Lewy
America in Vietnam. New York: Oxford University Press, 1978. A history that examines the charges against US military policy in the war and finds most of them unjustified.

Robert J. Lifton	*Home from the War: Vietnam Veterans, Neither Victims Nor Executioners.* New York: Simon & Shuster, 1975. Study of the psychological impact of the war on those who served there.
Myra MacPherson	*Long Time Passing: Vietnam and the Haunted Generation.* New York: Doubleday, 1984. The result of 500 interviews with people who "came of age" during the Vietnam war—those who served as well as those who didn't.
Allan R. Millett	*A Short History of the Vietnam War.* Bloomington, IN: Indiana University Press, 1978. Historical anthology about US involvement in Vietnam.
Richard M. Nixon	*RN: The Memoirs of Richard Nixon.* New York: Grosset and Dunlap, 1978. Includes excerpts from his private papers kept during the war.
Tim O'Brien	*Going after Cacciato.* New York: Delacorte Press, 1978. Brilliant, award-winning surrealistic novel of soldiers trailing a deserter who is "going to walk to Paris."
Carl Oglesby and Richard Shaull	*Containment and Change: Two Dissenting Views Of American Foreign Policy.* Toronto: Macmillian, 1967. Shows American "containment policy" to be a coverup for imperialism.
Norman Podhoretz	*Why We Were in Vietnam.* New York: Simon & Shuster, 1983. A conservative defense of US involvement in Vietnam.
Gareth Porter, editor	*Vietnam: A History in Documents.* New York: New American Library, 1981. A collection of official documents from both sides of the conflict from 1941 to 1975. Has excellent chronology.
Marcus G. Raskin and Bernard Fall, editors	*The Vietnam Reader.* New York: Randon House, 1965. An excellent collection of important documents, speeches, and articles as well as a thorough chronology of the war until 1965.
Harrison Salisbury, editor	*Vietnam Reconsidered: Lessons from a War.* New York: Harper & Row, 1984. Product of a symposium on the Vietnam war at the University of Southern California.
Al Santoli	*Everything We Had.* New York: Random House, 1981. An oral history of the war by the people who fought.

Robert Sheer	*How the US Got Involved in Vietnam.* Santa Barbara, CA: Center for the Study of Democratic Institutions and the Fund for the Republic, Inc., 1965.
Steven P. Smith	*American Boys.* New York: Avon, 1984. Novel exploring the attitudes and frustrations of four American "boys" who find themselves in combat in Vietnam.
Wallace J. Thies	*When Governments Collide: Coercion & Diplomacy in the Vietnam Conflict, 1964-68.* Berkeley: University of California Press, 1980. Claims diplomacy and force were not coordinated because of ignorance and bureaucracy.
Barbara Tuchman	*The March of Folly.* New York: Alfred A. Knopf, 1984. Devotes a long section to American involvement in Vietnam in a book exploring the question of why governments pursue policies harmful to their national interests.
James Webb	*Fields of Fire.* New York: Bantam Books, 1979. A novel showing a marine platoon which experiences a month of combat during which most are killed.

Magazines

The Angolite	May/June 1982. This Louisiana State Penitentiary inmate publication looks at the war from the perspective of veterans now in prison in an issue titled "Vietnam: A Criminal Legacy."
C. D. B. Bryan	"Barely Suppressed Screams," *Harper's,* June 1984. Discussion of several post-Vietnam books.
Fox Butterfield	"The New Vietnam Scholarship," *The New York Times Magazine,* February 13, 1983. Balanced overview of what recent scholarship says about the war and American involvement.
Mother Jones	November 1983. A special issue titled "Why Are We Still in Vietnam?"
The New Republic	May 3, 1975. A special issue titled "On the Disasters of the Indochina War."
Newsweek	December 14, 1981. A special issue titled "What Vietnam Did to Us."
Saturday Review	December 1972. A special issue titled "The Consequences of the War."

210

Index

The Editor

David L. Bender is a history graduate from the University of Minnesota. He also has an M.A. in government from St. Mary's University in San Antonio, Texas. He has taught social problems at the high school level for several years. He is the general editor of the *Opposing Viewpoints Series* and has authored many of the titles in the series.